Observer's Books

NATURAL HISTORY

Birds · Birds' Eggs · Wild Animals · Zoo Animals
Farm Animals · Freshwater Fishes · Sea Fishes
Tropical Fishes · Butterflies · Larger Moths · Insects
Pond Life · Sea and Seashore · Seashells · Dogs
Horses and Ponies · Cats · Pets · Trees · Wild Flowers
Grasses · Mushrooms · Lichens · Garden Flowers
Cacti · Flowering Shrubs · House Plants
Vegetables · Geology · Fossils · Weather · Astronomy

SPORT

Soccer · Cricket · Golf · Coarse Fishing
Fly Fishing · Show Jumping · Motor Sport

TRANSPORT

Automobiles · Aircraft · Commercial Vehicles · Ships
Motorcycles · Steam Locomotives · Small Craft
Manned Spaceflight · Unmanned Spaceflight

ARCHITECTURE

Architecture · Churches · Cathedrals

COLLECTING

Awards and Medals · Coins · Postage Stamps
Glass · Pottery and Porcelain · Firearms

ARTS AND CRAFTS

Music · Painting · Modern Art · Furniture · Sewing
Jazz · Big Bands

HISTORY AND GENERAL INTEREST

Ancient Britain · Flags · Heraldry · European Costume

TRAVEL

London · Tourist Atlas GB · Lake District
Cotswolds and Shakespeare Country

The Observer's Book of

LARGER MOTHS

R. L. E. FORD

DESCRIBING 94 LARGER MOTHS WITH
85 ILLUSTRATIONS IN COLOUR AND
74 HALF-TONES

FREDERICK WARNE

LONDON

Revised edition

© Frederick Warne & Co Ltd

London, England

1974

Reprinted 1978

ISBN 0 7232 1534 0

Printed in Great Britain by
William Clowes & Sons, Limited
London, Beccles and Colchester
527.878

PREFACE

It is not, of course, possible to study all the British moths in a work of this size, but it happens that all the larger moths, including those which fly in the daytime and those with the largest and most conspicuous larvae fall into the group termed BOMBYCES. It has been possible to include practically the whole of this important group in the book.

In addition to the BOMBYCES, eight species from the Geometrid and Noctuid Groups have been added to give some idea of what these large groups look like. Although mostly night-flying, they include very many fascinating moths well worth attention. Both groups, together with those missing from this book can all be found, fully illustrated, in the two volumes of Richard South's *Moths of the British Isles*, published by Frederick Warne & Co Ltd. For those wishing to know about the various techniques for studying insects in the field, there is now my comprehensive work called *Studying Insects*, also produced by the same publishers.

Richard Ford

INTRODUCTION

Moths belong to the large Order of Insects called Lepidoptera, and this order is divided into two divisions, Butterflies, or Rhopalocera, and Moths, or Heterocera.

There are other orders of insects, several of which are very much larger than that of the Lepidoptera, even in the British Isles, but it will be some time before the study of these other groups, and in particular the literature regarding them, makes them available for study and observations by a wider circle than serious scientists.

Owing to their size, moths were being studied long before strong pocket magnifying glasses came into general use and a great deal has been written about them. No doubt this gave an advantage to moths over the other orders, which require a microscope for the study of their smaller representatives, although when studied in detail other insects can prove as fascinating.

Although so much has been written there is still plenty to learn and record, and each year one or more new moths reach us from abroad, so that in time a good many of these species will become residents here.

The moths in the British Isles number over 2,200, and at present they are divided into ten Super-families. These are divided again into families and genera, and each genus can have one or many species.

There is a rough division made, which you may find used in literature, between the large moths, or Macro-Lepidoptera, and the small, or Micro-Lepidoptera, but

this is one of convenience for reference amongst collectors rather than a scientific classification.

Orders of insects are separated for a number of
reasons. One of the easiest to understand is the
difference in the life-cycle of insects of various orders.

A moth will lay eggs, which will hatch to caterpillars,
and these will turn into chrysalides. Finally the
chrysalides will become moths. The caterpillars in
the course of growing will change their skin several
times, and finally shed it to reveal a soft pale chrysalis,
which will harden and turn darker.

The Grasshopper, which belongs to the order
Orthoptera, will not have the same life-cycle. It lays
eggs which hatch into tiny grasshoppers, very like their
parents. These will grow and shed their skins, each
time becoming more like the adult insect.

Later in the text you will see that the scientific term
"larva" has been used for caterpillar and "pupa" for
chrysalis. The words "ovum", for egg, and "imago",
for the perfect insect, have not been used.

Moths can be separated from butterflies by their
feelers, or antennae. Butterflies have small clubs or
knobs on the end of their antennae, but the Burnet
moths, of which there are several different kinds, also
have a rather similar thickening at the end of their
antennae.

Later in the text both sexes of moths have been
referred to, and in some cases their different colouring,
or sexual di-morphism, has been described. In a
great many species, however, both sexes have the same
wing patterns and even exactly the same colouring.

The general appearance of the female may seem
similar at a quick glance, but a closer examination will
show that the body is generally much larger and that
the antennae are quite different. Those on the male

will be thicker and have a feathered appearance, while those on the female will be longer and thinner and will taper to a very fine point.

This is fairly distinct in most species, and you should learn to distinguish the sexes quickly so that a female can be saved from an untimely end and provide you with eggs. The hawk moths are rather harder to

Antennae of Butterfly   Antennae of Moth

tell by this method: generally their antennae look fairly smooth, but those of the female will be shorter and a little thinner.

BREEDING MOTHS. (With special reference to those described in this book.)

The life-cycle of a moth has been dismissed in a very few lines, in the belief that it is better to give details of the biology in the following pages, and in the text describing species rather than to give a more technical chapter on the anatomical changes and functions.

It is hoped those interested in moths will not be content to catch a specimen and possibly ascertain its name and then let it go, or even make a mere collection of rows of specimens correctly named. By obtaining eggs or by finding caterpillars and keeping them until they hatch out into moths you can have a very interesting and also instructive pastime. You will find yourself not only learning how some insects exist and what kind of moth a black furry caterpillar will produce, but also you will be learning the names of trees and plants and the types of soils on which they will grow.

EGGS

Most moths will lay their eggs in flat patches, and under a lens these will generally look like very small seed pearls. They can have a pearly lustre or a hard, solid appearance. They are generally round or slightly elongated. Those of the family Notodontidae are round and dome-shaped, with the flat side on the leaf on which they are laid.

The moths fasten their eggs to twigs and leaves by a thin sticky solution which coats the eggs and dries after they are laid. Those moths which lay their eggs in batches often attempt to conceal them, not perhaps purposely, but because by so doing many, many years ago some species obtained a better chance of survival and so the practice was passed on to their offspring.

The Satin moth coats its eggs with a white foam which dries and leaves the batch of eggs looking like a piece of white rice-paper; while some species coat their eggs with the tufts of hairs which were on their tails. This is a very effective method of disguise.

The larger moths, such as Hawks, will require much more food for their large larvae and are more careful with their egg-laying, and generally dot their eggs about in ones and twos.

Hawk eggs can often be found by bending back a branch so that the undersides of the leaves can be examined. You should, of course, be sure to look on the correct tree.

Most species of moth are very particular to lay their eggs on the correct food, and you should look on this for eggs; and what is more important, you should present the moths with suitable leaves or laying conditions if you wish to obtain eggs in captivity.

Most Hawks, while laying on leaves in the wild state, will lay just as well in a cardboard box, roughened on the sides to enable the female to crawl about.

Many of the species in this book will also lay in this manner, but in most cases their particular habit has been given. The Lackey moth must be given twigs to walk about on, since she will lay her eggs in a neat collar round a twig.

The Underwing moths like rough bark into which they can tuck their eggs. Frayed sacking is often favoured in captivity. There is a reason for this difference, and that is because this family will all pass the winter in the egg stage and the eggs must be dry and sheltered on a tree trunk.

If you catch a wild female moth she will most probably have been fertilized already by a male and will lay her eggs freely, but there are many kinds which, if they have not met a male, will lay infertile eggs which will not hatch. Such eggs will generally collapse and have a kink in one side and gradually dry up. A fertile egg will gradually change its colour, becoming darker as the time to hatch approaches. Finally the egg is often a dark purplish colour, and in the egg of the Hawk moth the young green larva can be seen curled up inside.

When eggs are obtained on leaves these should be kept in a small airtight tin, if possible with a glass top. They will not suffocate, and the leaf will remain fresher and keep the eggs moist. After hatching, the small larvae may eat or nibble their old egg-shells and then walk on to a fresh leaf which you have provided.

If you want to start collecting eggs begin with the Puss moth, which lays its eggs in pairs, one pair on a leaf and each egg just a little way apart. It is fond of small branches or shoots at the base of a poplar tree; it will be a chestnut red and quite easy to find late in May.

In the descriptions of each species later on, the time of year and egg-laying habits have been indicated in practically every case.

Lastly there will be a few moths which will never give you any eggs. Chief amongst these will be the Death's Head Hawk moth. I have yet to meet a man who can show me a specimen of this moth bred from the egg, even from eggs found in the wild state.

Larvae

There are many ways in which larvae can be collected. Most of those species described in this book have fairly large caterpillars, and some are very handsome and well worth keeping. Of course, sometimes a very exciting caterpillar produces a very dull-looking moth.

Many species have larvae which sit on the ground or on low-growing plants and sun themselves. This applies in particular to the furry kinds. Sunny days in the spring and a nice bank facing south are all that are required for an interesting walk. If there is a low thorn hedge at the top of the bank, with perhaps some ivy as well, so much the better.

A situation of this sort should produce Lappet caterpillars—but these are very hard to spot, sitting

INTRODUCTION

tight on a bare twig of blackthorn fairly low down—
Garden Tigers, Cream Spot Tigers, Drinkers, and
sometimes the smaller dark furry larvae of the Ruby
Tiger.

Later on these species can also be found, nearly
fully grown and much easier to spot, if you go out at
night with a good torch or lamp. Drinker moth
larvae can also be found at night feeding rather
noisily on reeds growing along ditches and dykes.

Larvae can be collected by "beating". This means
going up to the low branches of an oak or other suitable
tree and holding underneath it an open umbrella, up-
side down to catch things, and then tapping the
branches smartly with a stick. All kinds of life will
come down from the leaves, and amongst it you should
find some interesting larvae. Some of those kinds
which can be collected by this method are mentioned
later. The more serious collector uses a sheet of cloth
stretched out on a flat framework and known as a
beating tray.

Having found your larvae, you will have to look
after them properly and give them the correct food.

Small larvae hatched from eggs can be kept in airtight tins, which will keep the leaves fresh. Larvae
breathe through spiracles, which are the row of dots,
often white, down each side of the body, and the
amount of air they use is extremely small. It is not
necessary to punch great holes in a tin to let the larvae
breathe. This only lets the food get too tough to eat.

The cheapest cage is made by getting a few twigs or
sprays of food-plant and placing them in a paper bag
with the stalks sticking out. You can put in the
larvae and tie the bag up with string and place the
stalks in a jar of water. The disadvantage is that you
cannot watch their progress, unless of course you make

a cellophane window. Avoid a polythene bag, however, as these make condensation, which is very harmful. The method is not only useful in emergency, but is also very good indeed for a number of species.

The number of kinds of cages you can make or suitable containers you can use is legion and there is not space to detail them here. A few rules cover them all. You must have food fresh and not wilting, and you must have your cage tall enough to enable food to be kept with the stalks in a jar of water.

Don't forget to pack a little moss round the stalks to stop larvae which want to get to earth to pupate from drowning themselves.

Pupae

When nearing the time for pupation many larvae, particularly those of the Hawk moths, will change their colour from a green to a brown or reddish-brown. By this time you should have soft mould ready for them to bury in, at least 7 to 10 cm, and for some species moss should be placed on the top as well.

Large Elephant Hawk larvae will pupate just under the moss, while those of the Privet Hawk will burrow down nearly 30 cm into soil.

Puss moths and many others will require bark or a rough sheet of virgin cork to eat into before they make their cocoon.

If you keep larvae by the "sleeve" method—which means a long tube of stout muslin placed over a branch and tied at each end to form a cage with living food inside—you can sometimes place moss inside at the lower end and larvae will use this for pupation. If you do this, however, place a piece of old sacking round the outside to stop tits from pecking the pupae through the muslin.

Larvae do not like being disturbed when pupating. The larva first shrinks and becomes much firmer and shorter, and then the skin behind the head splits and slides down to the tail, leaving a soft pupa, which will soon harden and turn darker in colour. While in this condition it should not be disturbed or it will be damaged.

Many species pass the winter in the chrysalis or pupal stage, and if you have any in cages you can leave them where they are or dig the pupae up and place them in clean airtight tins. They should be kept cool and dry; a cellar is ideal.

In the spring they should be placed either on loose mould or on moss on loose mould with a little more moss on top of them. This can be kept damp by sprinkling with water. Moisture at the time of emergence is very important to all insects. You can warm them indoors if you wish, but don't place them in the sun to hurry them up or you may produce cripples.

Over your soil or moss you will have to place a few twigs and the newly emerged moth can crawl up these and hang downwards to allow its soft little shapeless bags to expand into wings. Allow plenty of room.

Collecting is a vast subject and hints on the various methods are scattered through the book. As such hints may apply to species in addition to those under which they are mentioned, it is advisable to read the whole text and to use the book for general reference afterwards.

The various techniques for collecting are more fully explained, with illustrations, in *Studying Insects* by R. L. E. Ford (Frederick Warne & Co Ltd). This book shows in detail, with drawings, how to make a simple but very effective cage. Frederick Warne have also published a *Hawk Moth Chart* illustrating 17 British hawk moths and their caterpillars in full colour.

INTRODUCTION

CONSERVATION

The Joint Committee for the Conservation of British Insects has prepared a code for insect collecting and

"believes that with the ever-increasing loss of habitats resulting from forestry, agriculture, and industrial, urban and recreational development the point has been reached where a code for collecting should be considered in the interests of conservation of the British insect fauna, particularly macrolepidoptera. The Committee considers that in many areas this loss has gone so far that collecting, which at one time would have had a trivial effect, could now affect the survival in them of one or more species if continued without restraint.

"The Committee also believes that by subscribing to a code of collecting, entomologists will show themselves to be a concerned and responsible body of naturalists who have a positive contribution to make to the cause of conservation. It asks all entomologists to accept the Code in principle and to try to observe it in practice."

Copies of the Code may be obtained from The Royal Entomological Society of London, 41 Queen's Gate, London, SW7.

LIME HAWK MOTH

Family SPHINGIDAE   *Mimas tiliae*

A fairly common moth, and more abundant near gardens in urban areas. Like other hawks, it is nocturnal, and is only seen in the day-time when at rest on fences or when drying its wings after emergence.

The adult moth emerges in early May and lays its eggs on lime or sometimes on elm. The egg

is almost spherical and pale green, and has a glossy appearance. The eggs are generally laid scattered about on the leaves fairly high up, and hatch in about ten days.

The larvae are pale green, but in the later stages some have handsome red stripes on each side. They have the curved spike or horn on their tail, which is generally pale blue.

When fully grown the larvae crawl to the ground to pupate. The pupa, or chrysalis, is in the soil a few centimetres down, or just under loose grass and can often be found by digging round lime trunks. The pupae have a rough

Lime Hawk Moth

surface and stay as pupae until the following
spring.

The illustration shows a typical female. The
colour of the moth varies considerably, and the
extreme forms are brick-red, deep green, or almost
black. The two spots can be reduced to a single
dot or enlarged and joined to form a band across
the wing.

Unfortunately lime and elm are the only food
of this species, and these will not keep very well in
water. Unless you have a growing tree it is not
easy to rear this species from the egg. If you can
use a growing tree, you can easily rear the larvae
by the "sleeve" method.

This means a stout muslin tube about 30 cm
wide and a metre long. Place this over a suitable
branch and tie the lower end securely round the
stem. Put in your young larvae and tie up the
top end. Don't crowd in too much food and
change to a fresh branch before the first is quite
finished, or the larvae will wander on the sides
and get pecked by tits. They should be removed to a cage with some earth in it when they
become dark, just before pupation.

POPLAR HAWK MOTH

Family SPHINGIDAE　　　　　　　*Laothoe populi*

The Poplar Hawk is one of our better-known hawk moths, but it is limited in its distribution by the food-plant—all species of poplar and also, but not preferred, sallow and willow.

The moths hatch in May, and can sometimes be seen attracted to lights, but they are only on the wing at night.

They vary in colour from light grey to very dark grey, and there are sometimes yellowish and pinkish forms, but these are not common.

The eggs are nearly spherical and a pale glossy green. These are laid singly on the leaves which will provide food. The young caterpillars are pale green, and the horn on the tail is also pale green. This colour remains for all stages of the larva, and it is only very rarely that you find a fully grown specimen with pinkish stripes along its sides.

The larvae of the hawks generally remain motionless during the day and feed at night.

Poplar Hawk Moth

They eat quite a considerable amount of leaves, so that the stripping of small branches can reveal their position to the knowledgeable collector.

When fully grown the caterpillars come down to the ground and make their chrysalis on the ground under turf or a little way into the soil.

Like those of the Lime Hawk, these can be found by digging close to the trunks during the winter months. They are dark brown and rough to the touch, and just over 2·5 cm long.

A male Eyed Hawk moth mated with a female Poplar Hawk can produce a hybrid similar to the Poplar Hawk but having eyes on the lower wings. These moths generally hatch the same year, about the end of September. They have been known to occur in the wild state and can be fairly easily produced in captivity.

Halved gyandromorphs also occur more often in this species than in most others. This means one-half male and the other female; and they can be detected by the different antennae, but more easily when each side happens to be a different shade of colour.

EYED HAWK MOTH

Family SPHINGIDAE   *Smerinthus ocellata*

The Eyed Hawk is often found in gardens where it will feed on apple trees. In the wild state it prefers sallow, but will also eat willow and poplar.

The moth emerges towards the end of May, and like other hawks flies only at night. When

freshly emerged the moth is a very handsome velvety insect and, of course, quite harmless to touch. The caterpillars of hawk moths all have a horn on their tails, but in spite of local rumours these do not sting and are perfectly safe to handle.

The eggs of the Eyed Hawk are nearly spherical and a pale glossy green. They will change to pink and grey just before the young caterpillar hatches out. The eggs are laid singly on the leaves of sallow or apple, and the young larvae are a pale green. When they are larger they can be distinguished from those of the Poplar Hawk

Eyed Hawk Moth

by the whitish appearance along their backs. They are also rough to the touch and during the day-time remain erect on a twig. Sallow shoots sprouting on the top of a hedge or bush, with leaves demolished by one of these caterpillars, can soon be detected.

A few of the larvae when in their last moult have pinkish lines along their sides, and their tail horns are more white than green in colour.

The fully grown larva descends to the ground to make its pupa sometimes as late as early September. The larvae of the hawk moths do not make an outer cocoon, but pupate in a small cell made by pressing out a hollow in the surrounding earth. The pupa of the Eyed Hawk can be distinguished from those of the Poplar and Lime Hawks by its smooth and shiny appearance. After coming to earth the fully grown larva will often wander a little way before making its way into the ground for pupating.

DEATH'S HEAD HAWK MOTH

Family SPHINGIDAE *Acherontia atropos*

Death's Head Hawk Moth

The Death's Head is the largest of the British moths, but is not a permanent resident here. It flies across from the Continent, generally in the spring, but the pupa cannot remain alive through the English winter, so the numbers will vary from year to year according to migrating conditions.

The name comes from the skull marking on the thorax of the adult insect. The moth can squeak quite loudly, very like a mouse, but is, of course, quite harmless.

The eggs are laid on potato leaves, and the entire plant will be eaten by one larva, leaving the bare stalks. The fully grown larva is very large, about 15 cm or more long, and has beautiful mauve stripes and black dots along its sides.

The moth flies some way after laying each egg and a number of larvae are hard to obtain from one place. The easiest way for a collector to obtain this species is to follow the potato-lifting machines and search for the pupae before the rooks find them. These pupae will not hatch in the open and are best placed in a flower-pot half filled with clean sand. A little clean moss should be placed on the sand and the pupa laid on top. The flower-pot can be covered with muslin and stood in a shallow saucer of water. The whole outfit should then be kept in a warm cupboard, in the dark, until the moth appears. This is often during October. The moss can also be sprinkled with water and the saucer kept filled. Once the pupa is allowed to get dry when heated, it will die.

Another tip for the collector is to search for the shrub called Duke of Argyll's tea rose, which has a narrow leaf and a pink blossom like a potato flower. These are often found at seaside resorts, and migrating females will be very likely to find them. The larvae are conspicuous, as they soon strip the long shoots.

CONVOLVULUS HAWK MOTH

Family SPHINGIDAE   *Herse convolvuli*

This grand hawk is not a resident but a regular
visitor to this island; it rarely succeeds in breeding
over here. The first arrivals come in June and continue until September, and have been reported from
many parts of the British Isles.

They are more often found along the south coast and
along the Essex side of the Thames estuary than elsewhere.

This hawk is also night-flying, but can often be seen
at early dusk flying and hovering over flowers. It
is attracted to sweet flowers, particularly honeysuckle,
sweet tobacco plants, and petunias; many people plant
beds of the flowers for the pleasure of seeing these
handsome insects. They can feed while flying by
thrusting the tongue (or proboscis) into a flower. This
proboscis is about 7·5 cm long, and when not in use is
coiled round under the head, almost between the eyes.

The larvae feed on the large convolvulus and are
brown with dark yellow lines along the sides. These
lines are continuous along the length of the caterpillar
and not short streaks as in some other hawks.

The pupae are remarkable since they have the
portion which houses the tongue separated from the
main body, and the result is very like a jug handle
fixed to the larger end of the chrysalis.

The easiest way to secure this species on the south
coast is to look along the eaves of beach huts during the
day-time, when the moths will be at rest.

Convolvulus Hawk Moth

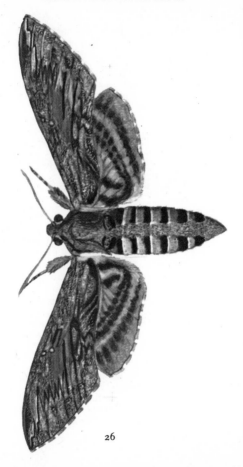

PRIVET HAWK MOTH

Family SPHINGIDAE   *Sphinx ligustri*

Privet Hawk Moth

A resident species which breeds here each year, the Privet Hawk, is also replenished by migrations from the Continent and is a fairly common species. It is found all over England and in southern Scotland.

This species emerges later than the other hawks, generally in June. The eggs are laid singly on the underside of leaves, and often many are laid on one bush. The food-plants are privet, lilac, and ash.

The Privet Hawk caterpillar is smooth and a handsome translucent green with short stripes along the sides. These stripes are really a double band, one of white and the other purple. The larva can be distinguished from all the other hawks at once, since the horn on its tail is a shiny black.

When ready to pupate, the larvae turn brownish, and they will wander quite a distance before burrowing into the earth. They also burrow deeper than other hawks, and if they are kept in captivity this point should be remembered. It is necessary to give them a large enough cage to avoid several burrowing on top of each other. The Privet Hawk chrysalis is brown and smooth and shiny. The part containing the tongue is raised up and almost separated from the body.

It now looks as if specimens which have been breeding for many generations in urban districts, especially in south-east London, are becoming darker.

A female moth is illustrated.

I have also seen one example of this moth which had the central black band on the hind-wing missing and replaced by pink. The larvae of this species are worth examining, as you may find one with two or more horns on its tail. These are in line, with the second one slightly smaller and behind the first.

PINE HAWK MOTH

Family SPHINGIDAE   *Hyloicus pinastri*

This species used to be confined to the pine-wooded areas of Dorset and Suffolk, and these were two distinct colonies. Today, however, the Dorset colony has spread along the coast and inland along the sandy areas where pine-trees abound, as far as Crowborough.

The Suffolk colony has also extended its area, chiefly southwards, so that the two colonies now almost overlap. Possibly this hawk is now most easily found in the Bournemouth area.

The Pine Hawk emerges at the end of June and is not a migrant species. The egg is more lozenge-shaped than round and is a shiny yellow, but turns grey before hatching. The eggs are laid along pine needles, sometimes two or three fairly close together.

The larva is green in the early stages and changes to dark green with brownish markings or to brown with reddish markings, and has a slightly oily appearance. It is quite distinct from the larvae of other hawks. The tail horn is dark brown.

The larvae will burrow in the earth to pupate,

but sometimes can be found under moss or a carpet of pine needles. The chrysalis is dark brown and very like that of the Privet Hawk, but the part housing the tongue is more roughened in this case.

The larvae will feed at different heights from the ground, but the moth is most easily found by searching the trunks of pine-trees during the day-time.

When fresh the moth is a dark grey, almost black, but this fades to a reddish-brown after a few days if exposed to light.

(*See also last paragraph on page 32.*)

SPURGE HAWK MOTH

Family SPHINGIDAE   *Celerio euphorbiae*

This species is a beautiful migrant hawk moth which visits England nearly every year, and would be plentiful if the food on which the larvae feed was more abundant. Unfortunately this plant, *Euphorbia paralias*, is not common and is restricted to a few areas.

The most famous locality is Braunton Burrows in Devon, and there is no doubt that the moth breeds there from time to time, although the early records lacked authenticity.

The moth emerges at the end of June or early July, and will fly both during the day and night-time. The eggs are laid on the food-plant, and sometimes several on one spray of the spurge.

The caterpillar is unlike most hawks and very pretty. The head is red, and the ground colour of the body is black, but this is almost entirely hidden by red or yellow dots. There are large spots on each segment of the larva, and these can be either yellow or red, each specimen having the spots all of the same colour. This alternative form of caterpillar occurs in several species of hawks.

The larvae burrow only slightly when fully grown and often merely get under loose grass and leaves. The chrysalis is very like that of the Large Elephant Hawk.

This is definitely one of the species which must have growing food for its larvae. Cut food in water renders the larvae liable to some illness, probably waterlogging, from which they will not recover. The Pine Hawk also suffers in the same way. Here, however, you can give cut branches which include a fresh growth on the end. Leave them, dry, in a cardboard box, and renew with fresh food about every three days.

BEDSTRAW HAWK MOTH

Family SPHINGIDAE   *Celerio galii*

The Bedstraw Hawk is an uncommon visitor from the Continent, and does not arrive here every year. Some years quite large numbers of them are recorded, and there is no reason why

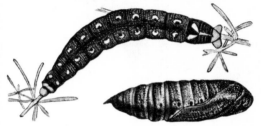

they should not survive our winter while they are in the pupal stage.

The moth reaches here in the spring and lays its eggs on the bedstraw, generally late in May. The larva is quite distinct from that of the Humming-bird Hawk, which also feeds on this plant.

The young larva is green, with yellow stripes down the back and sides, and has the horn on the tail tipped with pink. The larger larvae are distinctive, as they have a double row of large yellow spots down the back. The Spurge Hawk also has spots this size, but a double row down each side. The Striped Hawk sometimes has a row down each side of the back, but in this form the spots are divided by a bright yellow or pink line.

Bedstraw Hawk Moth

The spots on the larva of the Bedstraw Hawk are always present, but the ground colour can vary from black to various shades of purplish-grey and is sometimes green or brown.

The tail horn is pink, dotted with black and slightly rough.

The pupa is formed in the ground, and is brown, but usually the part containing the wings is of a different shade of brown; and the whole pupa is slightly rough to the touch.

The species is generally found round the coast, as the adults seem to lay eggs soon after arrival without penetrating further inland. The easiest way to obtain the species is to examine bedstraw by night with a torch. You may be lucky, but at least you should also find larvae of the Humming-bird and Small Elephant Hawks as well.

Rough ground on golf-courses and other open land is the best situation to search for the plants.

STRIPED HAWK MOTH

Family SPHINGIDAE   *Celerio livornica*

Another lovely immigrant hawk which arrives in June, or sometimes even earlier, and breeds over here. Fresh arrivals often continue to come up to the middle of September.

They do not come every year and not always in such numbers as to be easily found, but there have been notable years when this insect is fairly common along the south coast all the way from Kent to Porthcawl in Glamorganshire.

The larvae will feed on a variety of plants, the more usual being grape vine, fuchsias, dock, bedstraw, and antirrhinum.

The moth will visit sweet-scented plants at dusk, and males are also attracted to lights.

The larva is not unlike the dark form of the larva of the Convolvulus Hawk, but the ground colour is dark green, almost black, and the

35

narrow stripes which run from head to tail are yellow.

The pupa is formed on the ground under loose rubbish and emerges the same year unless formed too late in the autumn, when it will die as the cold weather approaches. This species is unable to survive the English winter.

This is not a species you can set out to find with any degree of certainty unless you devote a summer holiday to this end. Those fortunate collectors living on the south coast who operate light traps obtain the species fairly regularly, sometimes in small batches at a time.

LARGE ELEPHANT HAWK MOTH

Family SPHINGIDAE   *Deilephila elpenor*

A beautiful pink hawk moth which is very common in some areas, but you must know how to look for it. The moth is on the wing at the end of May and can be seen at dusk flying up

and down over patches of the greater willow-herb or fireweed.

The eggs, which are a pearly green, are laid under the leaves of this plant and sometimes more than one on a leaf. The larvæ will also feed on other species of willow-herb and on several other plants. These include fuchsia, evening primrose, virginia creeper and bedstraw.

The larvae are green in the early stages and in the last are generally brown, with four large eye-spots near the head. When disturbed these are brought into prominence by contracting the head back into the body, which expands the body and enlarges the eye-spots.

During the day the larvae are low down amongst the herbage, but at night they crawl up

Large Elephant Hawk Moth

to feed. If you examine a patch of willow-herb at night during early August you will find the fully grown larvae feeding near the top, and most conspicuous by torchlight. The moths are fond of damp places, and the larvae also like moisture. If you keep the larvae in cages with food-plant in a small pot of water, you should pack moss or something round the neck of the jar, or else the larvae will crawl down into the water and drown themselves.

The larvae are almost exactly like those of the Small Elephant Hawk, but of course grow very much larger.

They pupate on the surface of the ground under moss or rubbish. The pupae are a much lighter-coloured brown than those of the other hawks.

The moths became common in some parts of London, where the larvae fed on fireweed growing on demolition sites, even in the centre of the City itself.

SMALL ELEPHANT HAWK MOTH

Family SPHINGIDAE   *Deilephila porcellus*

This species is very like that of the Large
Elephant, but can be distinguished by the band
of yellowish colouring on the hind-wing, which
is between the pink along the edge and the dark,
blackish colour nearer the body. There are
similar yellowish markings on the fore-wings,
and the moth is also much smaller.

The Small Elephant Hawk is a native of this
country and extends to Scotland.   It is nocturnal,
and the larva also feeds at night. The easiest
way to find this insect is to use a lamp during
August and September nights and examine the
patches of bedstraw, on which it feeds.   The
larvae will then be browsing on the top of the
plant. They are quite conspicuous and show up at
once, but during the day they will be hidden well
under the plant.

The larvae are very like those of the Large
Elephant Hawk and have the eye-spots.   The
green colour is paler, and they also have the
alternative brown colour in the last stage.   They

do not grow anything like as large as those of the Large Elephant.

There is one peculiar and remarkable characteristic of the larva of this hawk, and that is its ability to feign death. In this species the larva not only remains quite motionless, even when

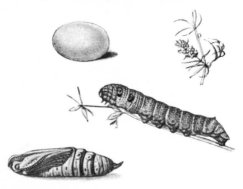

picked up, but can go quite limp and flaccid. When placed across a pin held horizontally the contents of the body hang down on either side in a limp bag and just the skin hangs across the pin. I have known experienced field workers pronounce a larva dead when shown this trick.

The favourite habitat is open ground, commons, heaths, and golf-courses, on which patches of white or yellow bedstraw flourish. The pupa is formed at the base of the plant under loose rubbish.

BEE HAWK MOTHS

Family SPHINGIDAE   *Hemaris fuciformis*
                                     Hemaris tityus

These two species are very alike when on the
wing, but have quite different feeding habits.
When at rest they can be distinguished from all
the other hawks by their almost transparent

Narrow
Hemaris tityus

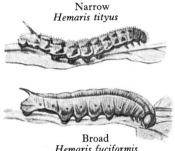

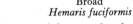

Broad   Broad
Hemaris fuciformis

wings, and from each other by the width of the
border round the edge of the wings.

Both moths are on the wing at the end of May,
but the Broad-bordered prefers drier country.
It can be captured when hovering over the flowers
of bugle. The flight is very fast and very like
that of a humble bee, except that at times the
moth can vanish in a fast swoop.

The Broad-bordered larvae feed on honeysuckle—not those clumps in woodlands, but
those on open ground, on the edges of rides, and
nice round clumps standing by themselves in the
open. The egg, which is pearly green and

41

Bee Hawk Moths

Broad-bordered

Narrow-bordered

almost round, is laid under a leaf. A freshly eaten leaf of honeysuckle will have a small rain-drop-like bead of juice on the edge of a feeding hole. If you find this, turn the leaf over and the larva will be resting along the mid-rib.

The Narrow-bordered Bee Hawk can also be caught on flowers, but the larvae feed on the devil's-bit scabious, which prefers moist situations, and grows almost flat on the ground.

The pupae of both species are formed beneath the soil. Like all hawks, they remain as pupae throughout the winter months.

HUMMING-BIRD HAWK MOTH

Family SPHINGIDAE   *Macroglossum stellatarum*

This species of hawk is unlike all the others in this country because it seems able to survive our winter as an adult. The moth's migrations from the Continent are frequent, and it has more than one brood here. The late broods emerge as late as the end of October, and in recent years there have been many instances of the adult succeeding in hibernating.

In the spring the eggs are laid on bedstraw during the day-time. This species is a day flier, but will also fly at night. They are lovely to watch as they hover over flowers of valerian, probing the blossoms with their long tongues. They make courtship flights up and down the faces of steep cliffs and road cuttings and the sides of large buildings, and pairing occurs in such places.

The moths are very strong and extremely fast fliers, and there is no doubt that they can cover long distances.

The larvae will feed on the bedstraw during the day as well as at night, and are green or pinkish grey. They are more easy to see during the night.

43

Humming-Bird Hawk Moth

During 1946 this moth was extremely common in some suburban areas, mostly in the south of London, where it fed on bedstraw growing on lawns that had been allowed to remain uncut during the war and in gardens of bombed houses.

The larva forms its pupa on the ground amongst rubbish, generally under the strands of bedstraw, and there is a very slight cocoon round the pupa case.

There are two main broods during the year, the first during June and the second at the end of September. There are other smaller broods between these dates from later migrants, the dates depending on the weather.

The adult moth can be distinguished from other hawks when at rest by its smaller size and very dark wings. These will be the fore-wings, which cover the hind-wings when at rest. If disturbed the hind-wings will prove to be pale brown.

Another method of catching this species is to plant a nice bed of tobacco plants in your garden. I think the plain white flowers have a slightly better perfume than the coloured varieties. This plant gives out a very sweet and pungent scent, and you can hatch Humming-bird Hawks during the day; and at night when the scent is even stronger you can watch for the Convolvulus Hawk, which will not settle but will plunge its long tongue straight into the flower while hovering.

ALDER KITTEN MOTH

Family NOTODONTIDAE   *Cerura bicuspis*

This moth, the smallest and certainly the most rare of the kitten group, emerges from its pupa and cocoon at the end of May and lays its eggs on birch and alder. The eggs are round, dome-shaped, and almost black, and are generally laid singly or in pairs.

The larva is green and has a yellowish-brown saddle type of marking down its back and two short tails side by side, pointing outwards. It cannot easily be confused with the other kitten moths, as they all feed on different food-plants.

The moth is scarce and only to be found in a few restricted localities and in small numbers, chiefly in parts of Sussex and in a few of the northern counties and the Lake District.

The first British specimen, a male, was found on alder, near Preston, in 1847. A second example was seen in the same locality two years later.

When fully grown the larva eats out a shallow depression in the trunk or branch of the tree, fairly low down, and makes a web cocoon over its back. Into the web it fastens all the sawdust from the excavation, and this hardens into a firm covering. The pupa is then safe inside. This will naturally match the bark on which it is made, and the pupae are very hard to find.

Before it emerges the moth spits out an alkali which softens the silk forming the matrix of the cocoon, and it then forces its way out.

Alder Kitten Moth

Unlike the other kittens this one is not quite so easy to find by looking for the eggs.   The trees are nearly always too tall, although sometimes small streams flowing through woods have the alders copsed along with all the other growth. This gives fine growth for a few years before becoming too tall.   Unfortunately the pupae get destroyed by the cutting process, but other moths will be in the area.

The alder often has minute pimples of a disease on the leaf and this handicaps the egg-searching when looking upwards.

The species comes well to mercury vapour light.   In fact, this method has shown the species to be more common than was first supposed.

In 1958 a young boy showed me a very fine variety of this species which I believe to be quite new.   It was almost entirely black on the fore-wings while the hind-wings were a very dark grey.   It was captured in Sussex with a mercury-vapour moth trap.

I have also seen a form in which the central black band was entirely missing.   This was also taken in Sussex, but quite a long time ago.

POPLAR KITTEN MOTH

Family NOTODONTIDAE   *Cerura hermelina*

This species is the commonest of the kitten moths and occurs in most districts where there are poplar and aspen. The moths emerge in June and are nocturnal. They can sometimes be found either when drying their wings after emergence, when they will be found a metre or so up the trunk of a poplar tree with their wings hanging outwards and downwards, or at rest on a tree trunk during the day. They will also come to a strong light at night.

The eggs are round, dome-shaped and practically black, and are laid in ones and twos on the leaves of the food-plant; they hatch in about ten days.

The larvae are similar to those of the Alder Kitten, but the marking from the head along the back is not continuous and there is a break behind the head and then a separate saddle-marking continued to the tail.

They are quite distinct from the Puss Moth, which is found on the same food, since the eggs are smaller and darker, and the young larvae are

Poplar Kitten Moth

not as dark. Also, the larvae of the Puss Moth have the dark colouring of the back joined to that on the head. The Puss Moth larva, of course, reaches a far greater size once it changes to its last skin.

The pupae are formed like those of the Alder Kitten just described, and are generally low

down on the trunk, often at ground level or just behind grass or foliage growing up against the base of the trunks of poplar trees.

There is usually only one brood in a year, but now and again there is a partial emergence of a brood, which does not always succeed in reaching the pupal stage, as it succumbs either to parasites or the weather in the autumn. The normal pupae remain until the following June.

SALLOW KITTEN MOTH

Family NOTODONTIDAE　　　*Cerura furcula*

The Sallow Kitten is not nearly as common as the Poplar Kitten, but probably far more widespread, owing to the fact that it will feed on all varieties of sallow. It occurs in a variety of localities, from mountain-sides to sand-dunes

and fens. The larvae will also feed on several varieties of willow.

The moth is on the wing in June and lays its eggs on the upper surface of the leaves, generally singly. The egg is like that of the other kitten moths, but quite black.

The larva is much paler than that of the Poplar Kitten, and the colour on the back and head is continuous along the whole length of the larva. The larva takes some weeks to become fully grown, and the pupae are more often found on the branches than lower down on the trunks of the trees on which the larvae have been feeding. The cocoons holding the pupae are similar

Sallow Kitten Moth

to those of the other kitten moths and very hard to find.   If they are on fairly thin branches they are often formed on the lower side of a fork, so that the larva takes advantage of the curve provided, and all that shows is a slight thickening of the junction of the branch to the main stem. Wild collected larvae or pupae of this species are very likely to be parasitized when found so that it is a better plan to search for the eggs.   In any case these are easier to find and can be seen by looking up against a strong light as well as looking down on shorter growth.

I have met collectors who have thought larvae of this species to be small larvae of the Puss Moth. There is a difference which will soon become apparent.   The Puss Moth larvae turn dark and then to a rich plum colour before they finally complete the cocoon.   The Sallow Kitten larvae turn a fine golden colour at this stage, and you should at once give them suitable twigs or cork for their cocoons.   There is nothing more annoying than a cage cemented shut by a cocoon of this group.

PUSS MOTH

Family NOTODONTIDAE   *Cerura vinula*

The Puss Moth is a fairly common species and also one which is very well known to most people; there are not many boys who live in or near the country who have not found or seen one of the fine larvae of this species.

The moth emerges at the end of May, and is almost white and very fluffy. It can be found on trunks of poplar trees during the day.

The easiest and the most interesting way to obtain this species is to search the young shoots at the base of a big poplar tree for the eggs. These are round, dome-shaped and dark red, and are nearly always laid in pairs on the upper side of the leaf. Besides poplar, the Puss Moth will feed on sallow and willow.

The young larvae are at first black, but soon change to a bright green with a black saddle-mark starting at the head and running the full length of the back to the tail which is two black spikes.

As the larvae grow these tails develop red, thread-like whips which can be extruded at will. These are used as whips to drive off flies which would parasitize the larvae by settling on them and inserting a sting through which they inject eggs. Grubs from these

Puss Moth

eggs would develop inside the larvae and ultimately kill them.

In the last stage the larva is a very fine insect, if not fearful. It grows fat and large, still a pale, almost transparent green colour, but the edges of the saddle-marking are now bordered with white.

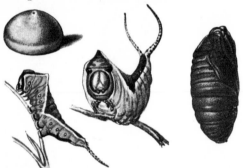

The head is surrounded by bright pink with two eye-spots, and the larva can draw back its head and the spots become more pronounced, so that it takes on a defensive frightening attitude.

The fully grown larva makes its cocoon like those of the kitten moths; it is most interesting to watch this process.

The pupa inside is almost black and seems very small for the size of the moth which will finally emerge.

In the illustration of the egg above, you can see a small opening at the extreme top. This is called the micropyle, and it is through this minute aperture that fertilization is able to take place, and it also allows the egg to "breathe".

It is also the weak spot, since there are two groups of hymenopterous parasites which oviposit in eggs, and their own eggs are inserted through this aperture.

LOBSTER MOTH

Family Notodontidae   *Stauropus fagi*

The Lobster moth is restricted in its distribution by the food which the larva eats. The chief food is beech leaves but larvae are not easy to obtain even in beech woods. There are other

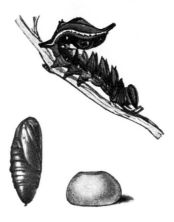

trees on which it will feed, but they are not the place to search with any degree of success.

The moths emerge at the end of May and lay their eggs on beech, oak, birch, and other trees. These are laid in small batches on the leaves.

It is the larvae from which this moth obtains its name. At first the young larvae look like the wood ant, but later develop into grotesque insects. They are a dark, rather shiny brown,

Lobster Moth

with the last segment blown out and held cocked over the back. The head of the larva is thrown back when alarmed and the legs are then spread out. It looks most uninviting to pick up.

In addition to the form of the moth illustrated, specimens occur in varying shades of grey to almost pure black all over.

The pupa is formed in a slight web between two leaves, and in some years there is a partial second brood.

When breeding this species you should allow the larvae to eat their egg-shells when hatching. Many collectors assert that this is actually essential. At any rate it is a well-established superstition. It is a most interesting species to rear but not always easy, and certainly does better on growing food than on cut food in water.

The adult has been found to come to a mercury vapour trap in a dark beech wood in the mid-afternoon.

MARBLED BROWN MOTH

Family NOTODONTIDAE   *Drymonia dodonaea*

This is a species which is found widely distributed, but nowhere in any large numbers.

The moth emerges in May and a second brood emerges in August. The eggs are laid on oak leaves, on which the larvae feed. The larva is green, with two yellow lines running down the back and also one along each side. The green is not a bright, clear green, but appears to have a whitish bloom over it, giving the larva a grey appearance.

The species is not easy to obtain, but the fully grown larvae can sometimes be beaten from the branches of oaks into a tray or open umbrella. The pupae are formed amongst the grass at the base of the trunks, and they can sometimes be found by searching at the foot of the trunks.

You will have to choose oaks in a large wooded area, as they are not found in residential areas or suburban parks.

A better way of obtaining the species is to beat the higher branches of oaks, which involves the use of a long ash pole and a very large sheet on which to catch everything. This has several disadvantages in that you require space under trees to operate and if possible clear ground for the sheet. However, if you have assistance from a party of collectors one can hold each corner and the sheet can be raised over obstructions. If there are only two people, then a pole can be fastened at each end as a stretcher and this can be held by an operator. The advantage of this method is that besides the enjoyment of collecting in sympathetic company there will be enough larvae to interest all, as one man's leavings will be another collector's prize.

This species occurs pretty generally over southern England, and as far north as Derbyshire, Westmorland and north Lancashire. It has rarely been seen in Wales and Scotland.

LUNAR MARBLED BROWN MOTH

Family NOTODONTIDAE   *Drymonia ruficornis*

A species very much resembling the previous one, but it is almost certainly single-brooded and the larvae take some time to become fully grown.

The moth emerges at the end of May, generally in the afternoon. It sits on the trunk of an oak tree to expand and dry its wings, and then ascends higher up into the tree.

The egg is pale bluish-white and round, dome-shaped like those of all the species in this family.

The larva is green, merging to bluish green on the back, with pale yellow or creamy white lines. The head is green and the mouth marked with pale yellow. It feeds on oak during June, July and August.

The pupa is deep reddish brown and is found in the earth at the foot of oak trees. It is possible to dig it out during the winter months. If you attempt this method you may find it disappointing at first, as it is possible to dig round many trees without finding a single pupa of any species. However, you may be lucky, for it is possible, on the other hand, to find thirty assorted pupae around one tree. Usually a tree standing a little away from any others will produce the best results.

This species comes well to mercury vapour light traps. Before the introduction of this method it was considered a difficult species to

Lunar Marbled Brown Moth

obtain. Results by beating were often most uncertain. Some fine melanic examples have recently been taken at light in Surrey. They are not unlike the Dusky Marbled Brown, but are, of course, larger.

The species is frequent in southern England, becoming scarcer northward. It is decidedly uncommon in Scotland. It occurs in Wales and Ireland.

SWALLOW PROMINENT

Family NOTODONTIDAE   *Pheosia tremula*

This prominent has two broods in a year, emerging as the adult insect at the end of May and again in August. It is fairly widely distributed all over England and parts of Scotland, but it is more easily found in the southern counties.

The egg is creamy white in colour and is laid on the leaves of the food-plants. These are aspen, black poplar, and several species of willow.

The larva is green, with a rather poorly defined yellow line down each side and, just above this line, a row of black dots. These are the breathing spiracles which all larvae have, but they are more noticeable when of this colour.

The larvae are also dimorphic, that is to say they have an alternative form of colouring, and this is a brownish colour all over. This dimorphism is found with many species of larvae.

The larvae are fully grown at the end of June and at the end of September, when they can be found by searching the leaves for feeding places.

59

Swallow Prominent

The pupae form in the ground, and have cocoons made from silk and particles of earth.

The species comes readily to light, sometimes in quite large numbers, and it is probably the best way to collect this and the next species, as you cannot be certain of beating larvae unless accompanied by a certain amount of luck.

If you try to obtain caterpillars of this species by pupa-digging, you should bear in mind that the second brood which will over-winter as pupae seem to have the sensible idea of burrowing much deeper than larvae of the first brood. You should also remember this when providing soil for bred larvae, since if this is too shallow the larvae bore down and then along the bottom of the container; and if you have a number they may all end up in a cramped heap together and you will get malformed pupae.

LESSER SWALLOW PROMINENT

Family NOTODONTIDAE *Pheosia gnoma*

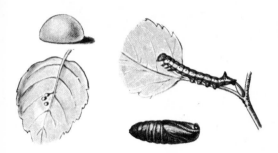

This species in the adult stage is very like the preceding one, but is smaller, and can be fairly easily distinguished by the larger and broader white wedge-shaped mark on the lower portion of the upper wings. This is shown well in the accompanying illustration.

The eggs are the same shape, round, domed, but are greenish white, and the larvae are quite distinct.

The larvae are purplish brown along their backs, with a yellow stripe along each side with black spiracles. They have a shiny or varnished appearance, which is an uncommon feature amongst larvae.

The food-plant is birch only, and the fully grown larvae are found at the end of June and at the end of September.

Lesser Swallow Prominent

The moth is on the wing at the end of May and early in June, and again at the end of July and in early August.

I have taken this species in north Kent. It comes readily to mercury vapour light traps, and follows on immediately after the emergence of the Swallow Prominent. The earlier emergences slightly overlap the last of the late Swallow Prominents.

This species seems to be more common in the north of England and in Scotland than elsewhere. It is also seen frequently in Ireland.

The species, in common with other prominents, is much subject to parasitism, and it is best to rear a series from the egg stage to avoid disappointment. There is a Braconid fly which will attack very young larvae and produce a batch of cocoons from the fully developed larva; and an Ichneumon fly which will attack the slightly larger larvae and which will emerge from the host pupa just when you were hoping for a moth.

PEBBLE PROMINENT

Family NOTODONTIDAE   *Notodonta ziczac*

This moth obtains its name from the round pebble-shaped markings on the tips of the fore-wings. This marking easily separates the species from all the other Notodontids. When the moth is at rest these marks resemble the broken ends of dead sticks rather in the same way as the markings on the Buff-tip moth.

The moth generally lays its eggs on the leaves of sallow or willow, but sometimes on poplar.

The fully grown larvae are a brownish grey, and like all those of this family look rather fatter at the tail end and have two warty humps on the middle of their back. These larvae are also inclined to walk humped up, rather like a looper caterpillar. There are tinges of purple on the humps and also just behind the head, which is green, and the last few segments of the body are yellowish brown.

There are two broods in a year. Moths are on the wing at the end of May and again at the end of July; larvae are seen at the end of June

Pebble Prominent

and at the end of August.   The winter is passed as a pupa in the ground.

The Pebble Prominent is widely distributed in this country, but is more easily obtained in marshy districts, probably due to the occurrence of a plentiful food-supply there.

In some districts darker forms may be found. In the typical form the female has browner hind-wings than the male.

This species comes readily to light.   In fact, all the prominent family can be thus obtained.

There is an interesting form of the Pebble Prominent to be found in the North of England and in Scotland.   This form is extremely dark; so dark, in fact, that the markings hardly show. Since it appears possible for this species to have a dark form it is quite likely that dark forms will occur in industrial areas further south, which follows the general pattern of events in a great number of species in recent years.

IRON PROMINENT

Family NOTODONTIDAE   *Notodonta dromedarius*

This species is one of the more common of the Notodontids and is widely distributed over the British Isles. The moth is on the wing at the end of May, but in some areas in favourable years there are two broods, and the second appearance is in August.

The larvae feed on birch, alder, and hazel. They are green, rather yellowish along the back, with a broad stripe on the back of the segments nearest the head and with purplish colouring on the humps on the back. In this species there are four of these humps along the back, the two end ones not being very pronounced.

The easiest way to obtain this species is by digging round the loose soil at the base of trees on which they feed. The pupae are dark brown and shiny, and are in a cocoon of silk and particles of the surrounding soil.

Iron Prominent

The form figured above is that usually found in the southern counties, but northwards the moth occurs in increasingly darker forms in which the reddish and yellow markings are much reduced. Dark forms of some prominents occur in Scotland and also in a few areas around Manchester.

Wild-collected prominent larvae are often much parasitized by a species of Apanteles, a Braconid fly, but pupae obtained by digging are generally sound.

GREAT PROMINENT

Family NOTODONTIDAE   *Notodonta anceps*

This species is the largest of the prominents and is fairly well distributed over the British Isles.

The moth is on the wing at the end of April until June, and is therefore earlier than the other species.   The moth comes readily to strong lights, which is the simplest way to catch it.

The larva feeds on oak from the end of June to early August.   The larva is green, sometimes a slightly bluish green with a whitish bloom on the back.   There are yellow lines along the back and seven reddish-yellow oblique streaks on the sides, similar to the streaks on the side of a hawk moth larva, except that they slope the other way.

When fully grown the larva becomes slightly purplish and makes a cocoon just in the ground at the base of the tree trunk.   The pupa is dark reddish brown and sometimes remains two or more winters before hatching out. This lying-over habit occurs in a number of moths and is a natural provision which enables them to by-pass a year. They cannot, of course, tell in advance that

there will be a drought or a heath fire which will destroy feeding grounds; it is entirely a haphazard occurrence, which, however, must play an important part in the survival of some insects.

This species was once regarded as rather a prize amongst collectors, but since the introduction of mercury vapour traps I have seen it in large numbers in Kent, Surrey, Sussex and Hampshire. However, it still remains a very handsome species to breed, with very fine larvae.

MAPLE PROMINENT

Family NOTODONTIDAE   *Lophopteryx cucullina*

The Maple Prominent is not rare, but is restricted in its numbers and distribution by the food-plant, maple, which grows on chalky soil mostly at the foot of the downs.

The moth emerges at the end of May and there is only the single brood. The eggs are laid on the leaves of maple, and the larva is one of the few species of large moths to be found on this tree and so cannot be confused with others.

The larva has a rather glossy appearance with whitish-green ground colour and with a darker green line along the middle of the back. There is a pale yellow stripe along the sides. There are no humps along the back, but one at the tail end of the larva. There are other variations in the larva and sometimes they are yellowish with purplish-brown markings and sometimes purplish with deeper purple markings.

If you obtain a larva with a humped tail similar to this on maple, you can be reasonably sure of your identification.

It is not an easy species to secure, as the numbers in any one area are not great. Pupa-digging in the winter yields the best results, especially if the trees are isolated ones. The pupa is just in the ground in a cocoon. These cocoons are, of course, harder to find than a pupa formed in the bare earth with no cocoon to surround it. It is very easy to overlook a cocoon formed in the

Maple Prominent

ground, especially as grains of earth will cling to the outside, often completely disguising the cocoon, but if you actually handle small, likely-looking lumps you will soon detect them. Pupae should not be removed from cocoons dug up in this manner, but left alone; otherwise you may expect crippled specimens. They should be kept fairly moist before and during emergence time.

COXCOMB PROMINENT

Family NOTODONTIDAE   *Lophopteryx capucina*

One of the commoner species of the prominents, but easily distinguished from all the others by the serrated edge of the fore-wings, which gives the moth its name. The actual colour of the moth varies considerably, but the serrated wings remain the same.

There are two broods, the first flying in May and June and the second in August. The species is widely distributed.

The larvae feed on a variety of trees, chiefly oak, beech, birch, hazel, lime, and aspen, but there are several others as well.

The larva is green, darker underneath, and with a darker line along the back. There are no humps on the back except a slight one near the tail. On this there are two bright red warts, side by side and quite small, which serve as an easy character for identifying the larva.

The general ground colour of the larva can also be brownish or purplish. The pupa and cocoon are formed in the ground.

In the northern counties there is only a single

Coxcomb Prominent

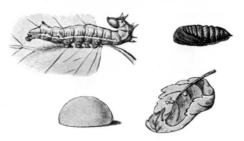

brood, and this is a feature with many of our moths. Larvae and pupae both develop more slowly in colder climates.

This species is now extremely common in some suburban areas and will come in large numbers to light. In these areas it is nearly always to be found on birch and lime.

Females may be found by examining fences, especially after a wet and windy night.

SCARCE PROMINENT

Family NOTODONTIDAE   *Odontosia carmelita*

This is another of the more uncommon prominents, but it has been found in small numbers from a great many places.

The moth emerges at the end of April and lays its eggs on the underside of the leaves of

birch, generally singly.   These eggs are round, dome-shaped, and pale blue.

The larva is quite distinctive, being green with darker green lines running down the back and sides and also with darker green rings running round the body.   These lines almost mark the body out in tiny squares of lighter green.   There is a yellowish stripe along the lower portion of the sides of the larva.

This moth appears to be restricted to one brood in a year.   The pupae form in the ground, in a cocoon, but they are too scarce to make digging for them profitable.   The best method of obtaining specimens is by beating the lower branches of birches for the larvae.

The adult moth may be taken at light, but females do not come easily by this method unless mercury vapour lamps are used.

Scarce Prominent

Pupae of this species should be kept in a cool place or they will emerge earlier than the normal time and you will have eggs hatching before food is available for the young larvae.

This species is not general over the whole of the British Isles. It occurs in Kent, Surrey, Sussex, the New Forest district of Hampshire, Hertfordshire and Berkshire. It is frequent in the birch woods of the English Lake District and on the "mosses" of the border country. It has also been reported from parts of Scotland and Ireland.

PLUMED PROMINENT

Family NOTODONTIDAE   *Ptilophora plumigera*

Male

Female

The antennae of the male of this species—
illustrated above—are plumed, which makes an
easy character for distinguishing them from other
Notodontids.

Unlike the other prominents, this species flies
at a different time of year, at the end of October,
and there is only the single brood.

The moth is fairly common, but mostly over
chalky districts where the food-plant, maple, is
to be found.

The moths prefer low-growing maples for
their eggs, and lay these on the twigs close to
the bud. Since these remain as eggs through the
winter, they can be found by searching.

The larvae are a bluish green, with a darker

green stripe along their back and whitish lines along the sides. The smaller larvae have yellow lines along their sides. The head is a yellowish green.

The larva has no hump on the back or tail, like the larva of the Maple Prominent, feeding on the same food.

Like the previous species, both sexes of the Plumed Prominent have rather thinly scaled wings which give them a slightly worn or shiny appearance.

This species was first recorded from Darenth Wood in north Kent and it may still be found there, but it may also be looked for along the whole of the range of chalk hills and anywhere south of the midlands where maple is found.

PALE PROMINENT

Family NOTODONTIDAE   *Pterostoma palpina*

This species is on the wing at the end of May and in early June, and has a second brood in July and August. Its colour makes it quite distinct from the other prominents.

The moth is fairly common in the south of England, becoming scarcer in the northern coun-

ties. It is easily attracted by lights and is otherwise seldom seen in the wild state as an adult insect.

The eggs are laid on the leaves of poplar, sallow, and willow. The larva is a bluish green with white or whitish-green lines along the back. There is a yellow line along the side and the uppermost edge of this line is black.

The fully grown larva makes its cocoon amongst the grass roots and dead leaves at the base of the tree trunk.

The pupae, which are fairly easy to find by

Pale Prominent

digging round poplar trees, are reddish brown, rather shiny and slightly smaller than most species to be found under poplars. These trees are of the best kind to reward pupa-digging attempts, as there are a number of species with sizable pupae which you are likely to find. Small lumps of earth should be examined or crumbled in the fingers to see that they are not cocoons disguised with grains of earth stuck to the outside.

Varieties of this species appear to be rare. There is a record of an almost black variety taken at Colchester, but no more have since been found. This form is similar to the form *lapponica*, which occurs in Russian Lapland.

There is also a minor variety which has been named *ab. fasciata* by Cockayne, and this form has a brown fascia.

If this species were to be reared in some numbers, then some more of these and other forms would no doubt appear, but collectors seem content to take an easy series from light traps rather than go to the trouble of breeding.

BUFF-TIP MOTH

Family NOTODONTIDAE   *Phalera bucephala*

A very common moth and easily found in suburban parks and gardens, where it generally feeds on the lime trees. In the wild state it is more commonly found on oak, sallow, birch, and other trees.

The moth is on the wing towards the end of June. When at rest it closely resembles a short piece of broken birch twig; it is also not unlike a cigarette end! The wings are folded up over the back so that the moth is then stick-shaped.

The eggs are laid under the leaves of the food-plant and in a large batch. They are small, for the species, and white.

The larvae all keep together even when fully grown, and they can be seen in clusters on branches which they have stripped of their leaves.

The larvae are mainly yellow, with black markings and a black head. They are covered with a fairly long white down, and if a group of them is disturbed they will all drop to the ground.

The pupae form in the earth, without a cocoon, and they are dark brown and shiny.

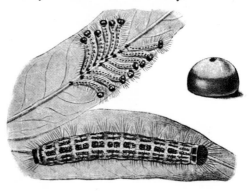

As soon as the larvae hatch from the eggs they eat the lower side only of one leaf, generally that on which the eggs were laid. This leaves the leaf white all over and makes it easy to see on lime trees in suburban areas during the last weeks in July. Young larvae are more trouble to collect than fully grown ones later, but they will be free from parasites.

The late Mr. H. D. Swain, who painted the beautiful coloured figures for this work, caught a unique chocolate-coloured variety of this moth, and it is now in the national collection.

CHOCOLATE-TIP MOTH

Family NOTODONTIDAE   *Clostera curtula*

This moth is not abundant, though it is widely distributed. It is on the wing in April and May, and there is a second emergence in July and August.

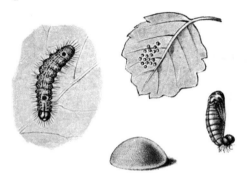

The eggs are a curious bright verdigris green and they are laid in small batches on the leaves of poplar and aspen.

The larvae feed at night and during the day stay in a house spun from leaves. This is very like a box, one leaf rolled for the sides and either a portion of the same leaf or a second leaf spun across the two open ends to close them up.

The larva is rather hairy, grey, with small black markings and with orange spots on the sides. On the fourth segment and also on the eleventh, at the tail, there is a small raised spot,

Chocolate-Tip Moth

coloured black. The pupa forms amongst spun leaves similar to the box in which the larva feeds.

Richard South, writing nearly seventy years ago, says this species appears less common in England than formerly. Although I have found the larvae abundantly in a few places, they are frequently highly parasitized by a species of Tachinid fly which seems to be able to get at them, although the larvae stay boxed up in their cells during the day.

I have found pupae of this species inside their boxes on the growing plant in late September. Presumably these leaves will drop to the ground later and the moth will emerge in the following spring. Mine emerged successfully, much to my surprise, as I thought that normal larvae might pupate elsewhere for the winter and these might be parasitized ones, which often have a different behaviour from healthy specimens.

CHOCOLATE-TIP MOTHS

Family NOTODONTIDAE

Scarce
Clostera anachoreta

Small
Clostera pigra

These two species are both on the wing at
about the same times, at the end of May and
again in July. Sometimes the second brood of
the Small Chocolate-tip is later, even as late as
October.

The larvae of both species feed in the same
manner, just described, in a box of leaves. The
food-plants for both are poplar, willow, sallow,
and aspen. The Small Chocolate-tip is more
easily found on *Salix repens*, where this occurs.

The pupae are formed in a box made from
leaves, and when on sallow these will often stay
on the twigs during the winter, and may easily be
found by searching.

These two species have been hybridized many
times, but there is nothing spectacular in the
result. The offspring more closely resemble the
female of the species which produced them.

The larvae of these two are very similar, but
the Scarce Chocolate-tip larva has the raised

spots on its back reddish brown or red, and the larva of the Small Chocolate-tip has the raised spots coloured black.

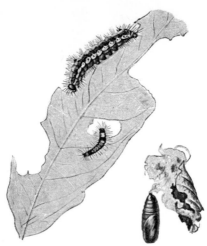

The moths, although similar, can be distinguished fairly easily, as the Small Chocolate-tip, besides being smaller, has a less distinctive chocolate tip to the wings, the marking being more blended into the ground-colouring.

The Scarce Chocolate-tip is a rare species recorded mainly from the coasts of Sussex and Kent. The Small Chocolate-tip is widespread almost throughout Great Britain.

BUFF ARCHES MOTH

Family NOTODONTIDAE   *Habrosyne derasa*

This is a beautiful moth and widely distributed over most of the British Isles, although not occurring in great numbers in any one place. It prefers well-wooded districts.

The moth is on the wing at the end of June, but in some years specimens can be caught in late September. This is a partial emergence and not a proper second brood.

The larvae are a rusty brown, with a blackish line down the centre of their backs. They feed at night on bramble and low-growing bushes, and in captivity will also eat raspberry canes.

The pupa forms in the ground or amongst rubbish, and is enclosed in an earthen cocoon.

The easiest way to secure this moth is by the treacling method.

Another extremely powerful attraction is the essence of the Jargonelle Pear. Unfortunately the real oil is extremely expensive, but a very good substitute is the common "peardrop" or amyl acetate, which is easy to obtain and very cheap. This can be added to the tin of sugaring mixture, but use only a few drops or you will defeat your object and repel insects.

The adults also come well to light traps, being among the earlier arrivals, but they are rather inclined to be fidgety and may damage themselves before they have time to settle down.

It is a most attractive species to breed. The pupae remain conveniently in this stage over the

Buff Arches Moth

winter months and the beauty of the moth when freshly emerged makes the effort well worth while.

There have been no records of any variation in this species other than the slight differences in the general ground-colour.

The moth also extends across Central Europe and eastwards to the Himalayas, Japan and Korea.

PEACH-BLOSSOM MOTH

Family NOTODONTIDAE   *Thyatira batis*

Possibly the most beautiful of this group of moths, the Peach Blossom is a magnificent insect when freshly emerged. I have seen as many as twelve at a time crowding on a treacle patch, and it is an inspiring sight.

The moth emerges at the end of May and lays its fluted, greenish-white eggs on the edges of bramble leaves, on which the larvae feed. The larvae are light reddish brown, with a thin line of darker brown down the back and a broader one along the sides.

There is a slight hump on the back close to the head and one at the tail. There are five more along the back, but these are divided slightly, into two ridges.

When at rest the hind claspers are often held clear of the twig or ground and do not grip anything.

The larvae feed to their last stage irregularly, so they end up by pupating at different times. There will be some which will emerge as a partial second brood at the end of August, while the others will pass the winter as pupae.

Peach-Blossom Moth

They make their cocoons among loose leaves at the bottom of the plants. The species inhabits well-wooded country and is most easily obtained by the treacling method.

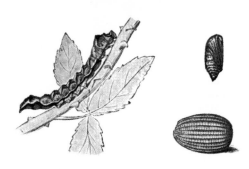

I have yet to see an extreme variation of this species but there is quite a pretty form which can be found. It has the two spots on the wing-tips enlarged and more confluent than in a normal specimen.

FIGURE OF EIGHTY

Family NOTODONTIDAE   *Tethea ocularis*

This species obtains its name from the whitish marks on the band across the fore-wings, which resemble the figure 80.

The moth is fairly widely distributed, but is not found commonly anywhere. It emerges at the end of May or during June and lays its eggs on the leaves of poplar trees, generally in very small batches well scattered about.

The larva feeds between two leaves fastened together but left quite flat, and, surprisingly enough, it is quite easy to find with determined searching.

The larva is yellowish, rather grey on the back, and with an orange head. There are other minor black markings, but no other caterpillar feeds in the same manner on the same tree except the one next described, and that can easily be separated because it has a dark line down its back.

The larvae are inclined to take their time over growing up, and when fully grown develop into pupae inside a very slight cocoon between two leaves. The pupa is a shining black.

Possibly the easiest way for the collector to obtain this species is by sugaring the poplar trunks at the end of May.

The moth also comes very readily to mercury vapour moth-traps and in some favourable areas will appear in quite large numbers, although otherwise it is seldom seen.

Figure of Eighty

Since this method of obtaining this species was discovered the larger numbers examined have shown that quite a range of variation can be expected, as entirely black specimens have been found. These still have the whitish figure of 80 showing.

POPLAR LUTESTRING

Family NOTODONTIDAE   *Tethea or*

This moth is out later than the species just described, flying in June and July, and except for the missing 8o is not unlike that species.

The larva feeds on the same food-plant, poplar, and in the same manner between two leaves left quite flat.

The larva is not quite so whitish, but is a pale yellowish green, with a dark line down its back. The pupa is formed in a slight cocoon in the same way, but in colour this is reddish brown rather than black.

The distribution of this moth is about the same as that of the preceding species, but both are quite hard to come across.

South says it comes freely to sugar, but that it is not easy to box. Some moths drop to the ground when a light is shone on the sugar patch to which they have been attracted, but others fly off, sometimes returning for more and thus giving you a second opportunity to capture them. For these species I use a little more alcohol in the treacling mixture and they get tipsy or drowsy and easy to catch.

Poplar Lutestring

If you obtain a female by the sugaring method you can rear a brood from the eggs. You should, however, allow them ample food as each larva will require two whole leaves to itself which it will fasten together face to face so that they remain flat. If they are overcrowded so that one caterpillar has to eat the house of the next, they will be disturbed constantly and will spit. Many species of larvae spit when disturbed. This means that a blob of fluid appears round the mouth-parts, and it is not projected. Some species like the Double Lunar Stripe eject a big blob of fluid and can then suck it in again provided it does not become smeared about in the meantime. However, the general opinion is that spitting caused by overcrowding also aids disease and should be avoided.

If you are unable to obtain eggs you can sometimes find the larva by standing under a pollarded poplar and seeing it, lying between two leaves, against the light.

COMMON LUTESTRING MOTH

Family NOTODONTIDAE   *Tethea duplaris*

The colour of this moth varies considerably, the most extreme being practically black, so that you may have some difficulty in identifying it from a captured specimen.

The moth emerges in June and July and is very widespread in its distribution. In some areas it is fairly abundant.

The larva feeds on birch, making a slight web with a few leaves which conceal it during the day-time when it is at rest. It comes out of this at night to feed, and the collector can then obtain it by the beating-branches method, during late August or September. During the day the larvae cannot be dislodged from their leaf-shelter.

The larvae are greenish, with different shades of green in lines down their sides. Their heads are reddish brown, with black marks.

The pupa forms between spun leaves and is a dull reddish colour.

Besides birch, which is the usual food-plant, this species is sometimes found on hazel, alder, and oak.

Although smaller in size the male of the Common Lutestring Moth might easily be taken for a slightly worn specimen of the Satin Lutestring Moth as the markings are very similar.

The female Common Lutestring Moth, has not such a distinctive dark central band.

The outer edge of the dark band has two black

Common Lutestring Moth

dots and if the specimen is not worn it can easily be distinguished from the following species by these spots.

In Scotland and northern England the general ground-colour is blackish or purplish grey, so that this results in a more or less uniform dark colour.

The species is quite common in most woodlands, especially in the south and east of England, and is distributed through Scotland to the Shetlands. It has also been found in many districts in Ireland.

SATIN LUTESTRING MOTH

Family Notodontidae   *Tethea fluctuosa*

This species is very like the one just described, but the average specimen is slightly larger and the markings are very much bolder and better contrasted. The ground-colour is also much whiter and not yellowish.

It is distributed over most of the British Isles, in restricted areas, but is quite rare. It is rather easier to find in the southern counties.

The moth emerges in June, and lays its eggs sparingly on birch.

As in the previous species, the larva hides in the day-time amongst spun leaves and comes out to feed at night. The larva is reddish grey on the top and yellowish white underneath, so it can easily be distinguished from the larva of the Common Lutestring Moth, feeding on the same tree in the same manner.

The pupa forms amongst spun leaves, but not always on the tree. The larvae feeding in late September will often descend to the ground and spin their slight cocoon amongst fallen leaves.

Beating at night for an uncommon species is

Satin Lutestring Moth

hardly profitable, and the best method of seeing this species would be by attracting the adult moth to light.

The moth will come to mercury vapour moth-traps, but as stated earlier it is rare and only to be found in small numbers although it seems to be fairly evenly distributed over the countryside.

The moth is rather more handsome than the other species closely related to it, as the markings are bolder and much more distinctive and it is very pretty when freshly emerged.

OAK LUTESTRING

Family NOTODONTIDAE   *Asphalia diluta*

The adult moth of this species is fairly distinctive and you should have no difficulty in recognizing it from the illustration.

The moth flies in late August or September, and will come very readily to sugar patches on oak trunks.

The moth is most commonly found in the southern counties, but is also fairly distributed elsewhere.

The larvae feed on oak during May and June and, like the previous species in this little group, feed only at night and hide amongst spun leaves during the day-time.

The larva is yellowish on top and darker or greyish underneath, with a line down its back and another line, dotted with black, running along each side fairly low down. The head is a very dark brown.

The chrysalis is reddish and is enclosed in a slight cocoon amongst leaves.

The moth varies quite considerably, and this applies to both males and females. The chief variation is in the width of the two dark bands on the fore-wings and in extreme cases these bands nearly meet each other to form one wide one.

Besides this variation in the widths, the colour of both the bands and the ground-colour can vary. There is a local form which has this darker colouring to which is added a dark patch next to the thorax on the fore-wings and three

Oak Lutestring

cross bands of reddish or purplish brown.   This was first found in Yorkshire where it is still taken.

The species is more common in England than in Wales, though it is fairly widely distributed throughout both countries.   It is also found in southern Scotland, but not in Ireland.   It extends across Central Europe and to the north-eastern parts of Asia Minor.

YELLOW HORNED MOTH

Family NOTODONTIDAE   *Achlya flavicornis*

This moth is a most interesting species which emerges very early in the year, generally in March or April, and before the leaves are on the birches on which it feeds. The moth flies at night and remains at rest on birch twigs during the day. Since there are no leaves on the trees, it is quite conspicuous and easy to find. It will also be at rest on posts and trunks, but it is most noticeable on very young birches. The weather at the time may be severe, and these moths have been seen when there has been snow on the branches.

The larva is very large for the size of the moth it produces. It is various shades of green on top and yellowish underneath, with rows of black dots on each segment. The dots on the upper side of the larva are white-centred. The larva is quite a distinctive one. It feeds only at night, hiding in the day amongst a shelter of spun leaves.

The young larva folds a leaf in half and hides inside, and in this stage is almost black. The fully grown larva forms its pupa on the ground

Yellow Horned Moth

amongst leaves, moss or grass roots, with a very slight protecting cocoon.

The moth is well distributed and very common in some birch-woods and on commons with small or young birches.

This species is variable and I have seen some fine black-banded specimens and some almost entirely black. It would be well worth collecting the species from a number of different areas to establish the range of variation.

FROSTED GREEN MOTH

Family NOTODONTIDAE   *Polyploca ridens*

Like the Yellow Horned, this species is also
out very early in the season, being fairly easy to
find sitting on the trunks of oak trees during the
day-time. If the trunks are green or covered
with moss and lichen the moths will be almost
impossible to find. Tree
trunks of up to 12–15 cm
thick can be jarred quite
easily by a hard kick with
the heel of your shoe.
Although you won't see the
tree move, there is vibra-
tion which can be sensed
by insects sitting on the
trunks, and they will take
to flight. You have to be
pretty nimble to net them.

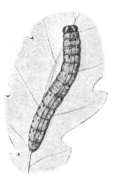

Another method is to use
an ordinary bee-smoker
and puff smoke out, which will immediately
disturb insects at roost. Smoke is a great aid to
collecting, and if you carry a tube such as the
handle part of a bicycle-pump, and insert this
into the base of a huge clump of grass and then
blow cigarette smoke down it so that the smoke
goes in at the middle and drifts outwards, all
insects will leave—even beetles.

You will be unpopular if you try this on Forestry
Commission land, where smoking is forbidden—
and quite rightly so.

Frosted Green Moth

The larvae feed on oak, generally the lower branches of large trees rather than on small oaks. This makes them rather easy to obtain by the beating method. They hide among leaves in the day-time, but are not fastened in by web, so that they can be freely knocked out.

The larvae are yellow on top and greenish underneath. There is a greenish-grey double stripe along the back which is not continuous where the segments meet. The head is yellowish, with a black mark on each side, and it is dented at the top so that if seen from directly in front it appears heart-shaped.

The moth flies in April and the larvae can be found in June and July. The species is widely distributed, but most common in the larger oak woods in the southern counties. This species has also been recorded from Wales and also as far north as Cumberland, where the adult moths are rather darker in appearance.

Apart from this geographical difference in colouring there have been no extreme varieties of this species recorded.

VAPOURER MOTHS

Family LYMANTRIIDAE

Vapourer male   female
Orgyia antiqua

Scarce Vapourer male   female
Orgyia recens

The Vapourer Moths are the only two in this group which have females with no proper wings. They are shown beside the males, and look very much like spiders with extra-long bodies. The females are very much larger than the males and are really nothing more than walking egg-containers.

Both species fly in June and have a second brood later on. They are quite hard to find in the country, especially the Scarce Vapourer, but the Common Vapourer has become urbanized and is abundant in gardens and parks in towns, even in the heart of London.

Vapourer Moths

Both species will feed on a great variety of trees and plants.

The larvae are dark and thinly covered with fairly long hairs, and there are tufts of dense hair at the head and tail and four stiff brushes or tufts of hair in the middle of the back, nearer the head than the tail. These tufts are yellowish and there are red dotted lines along the sides. There are other markings, but the larvae are most difficult to recognize from a description.

 The larvae which will ultimately be females are much larger, and all shed their hairs, which are incorporated in the web forming the cocoon. The female cannot, of course, fly, and she often lays her eggs on the outside of the cocoon.

These eggs are in a flat patch, and are round with the centre slightly indented. In London those of the Common Vapourer can easily be found on the trunks of trees in the parks.

The males of the Vapourer fly in sunshine, and that of the Common Vapourer looks very golden in the sun. It flies not unlike a butterfly, and I have often been told that collectors have seen a "Large Copper" flying, sometimes in towns!

DARK TUSSOCK MOTH

Family LYMANTRIIDAE   *Dasychira fascelina*

This is an uncommon species and inclined to be restricted to certain areas.   It is fairly easy to find in some coastal areas, but there are also one or two strong colonies well inland.

The moth emerges in June or July and lays her eggs on sallow, broom or heather.   These eggs are slightly sticky and hairs from the tuft on the end of the female abdomen adhere to the eggs and help to conceal them.

The larvae when fully grown are most handsome, being dark and hairy, with five dense tufts of hair along the back, which are white, with the tips black. There is also a smaller tuft pointing outwards from the head and tail.   These larvae are distinct from any others in having black and white as their only colours. When touched they will coil up; this makes them rather easy to beat from broom or sallow.

The larvae make a cocoon, and the pupa inside is black and also hairy.

It spends the winter as a small larva which hibernates in a small silk cocoon, generally fastened to a branch, where it remains until April or May, when it quickly becomes fully grown.   Young larvae, produced from a batch of eggs, can be kept during the winter months of

Dark Tussock Moth

Male

Female

hibernation by sleeving them in a tube or sleeve of stout muslin tied over a branch of a growing broom. This is especially effective if the broom is an old branch which has been cut in mid-summer after flowering and allowed to sprout a rather thick growth.

On Dungeness, which used to be one of the haunts of this species, the broom plants grow flat along the shingle, partly due to the prevailing wind. If you gently tuck a sheet under these plants and then shake them, you will find the larvae if they are about, since they coil up and drop off the plant.

PALE TUSSOCK MOTH

Family LYMANTRIIDAE   *Dasychira pudibunda*

Male

Female

Also known by other names, generally the Hop
Dog, this is a common species well distributed
throughout most of England and Wales.

The moth emerges in May and June and lays
its eggs in a batch, generally on branches or
trunks rather than on leaves.

The larva is very handsome and quite distinctive. It is very hairy, pale green or pale yellow;
along the back there are four thick brushes of
yellow hairs and at the tail there is a tuft of red
hairs. When these larvae roll up, as they will
do when disturbed, the skin between the segments
will be stretched, and this is a shiny black.

Pale Tussock Moth

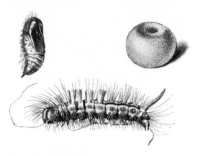

The larvae feed on a number of trees, chiefly elm, oak, birch, and hazel, and also cultivated fruit-trees and hops.

The pupa is hairy and is enclosed in a web cocoon, generally in a crevice in the bark.

The easiest way to obtain this species is to search tree trunks for the females and breed a series from the eggs. The beautiful larvae are well worth the trouble.

In recent years some evidence of industrial melanism has been apparent in this species and some dark forms have been found, including some with fine dark bands, especially in the male. No doubt, with breeding, pure black strains could be produced, but before long these may appear in suburban areas.

YELLOW-TAIL MOTH

Family LYMANTRIIDAE   *Euproctis similis*

A common moth found over most of England, but the larva is probably better known than the moth on account of its attractive appearance and habit of sitting about on leaves sunning itself, which makes it rather conspicuous.

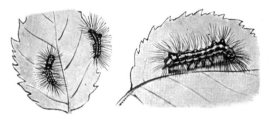

The moth emerges in June and July, and sometimes there is a partial second brood emerging in September.

The eggs are laid in a batch covered with the yellow hairs from the tail of the female.

Unlike those of the Brown-tail, these larvae feed singly and, when small, hibernate in pieces of curled leaf, fastened with silk. In the spring they feed voraciously and will eat most hedgerow shrubs and also garden roses and fruit-trees. They are never very abundant anywhere, but most large hawthorn hedges will produce a few.

The fully grown larva is black, with black and grey hairs with a scarlet stripe down the middle of the back, and on each side there are tufts

Yellow-Tail Moth

of pure white fluffy scales. There is no other larva quite like that of this species.

The pupa is formed in a cocoon made from web and incorporating the hairs and scales from the larva.

The hairs of this larva, like those of many others, will stick in the pores of the skin, especially the softer parts between the fingers, and may cause an irritation. This urtication is more severe with the larvae of the next species.

Although widely distributed so that an odd specimen can be found anywhere, you are not likely to obtain a series unless you try beating a fairly unkempt hedge of mixed growth in May. This should produce fully grown larvae which do not cling when disturbed but curl up and easily fall on to your beating tray or inverted umbrella.

A female moth is illustrated.

BROWN-TAIL MOTH

Family LYMANTRIIDAE   *Euproctis chrysorrhoea*

This is another species which is better known from its larvae. Although this species is quite widely distributed, it is found in fairly restricted colonies, sometimes quite small ones. On Canvey Island the insect simply swarms over every bush and tree, sometimes completely de-foliating whole clumps of bushes and moving on to the next.

The larvae make a small silk tent in which they hibernate. They make a larger one the following spring; they sun themselves on the outside and shelter inside and also cast their skins there. Some bushes become so white with webs it looks as if laundry is spread out to dry.

The fully grown larvae are not gregarious and disperse to find food.

The larvae feed on hawthorn, blackthorn, and sea-buckthorn as well as other trees. In America, where they are a severe pest, they even eat conifers.

The larvae are similar to those of the Yellow-tail, but the markings are much more blurred.

Brown-Tail Moth

They can be easily distinguished by their web tents. The hairs are extremely urticating, especially to some people. On a windy day when the fully grown larvae start to shed their hairs it is advisable to keep well away from bushes on which they have been feeding.

The pupa forms inside a silken cocoon.

Although this species is more widely distributed in Essex, and sometimes even gets reported in the newspapers as an army of caterpillars fought with flame-throwers, it is inclined to keep to very small compact colonies in other areas. There are a number of these along the South Coast, including one below the Buddle Inn, at Niton, I.O.W., and another on Dungeness. The Kent colony produces a form with small black dots on the wing.

A female moth is illustrated.

WHITE SATIN MOTH

Family LYMANTRIIDAE *Leucoma salicis*

This moth is pure white all over. A female is illustrated here. There is a rare casual migrant species, about the same size or larger, which has a dark mark on each fore-wing. This is *Leucoma v-nigrum*, the Black V, and there is no reason why this should not become established here.

The White Satin emerges in July and August and lays its eggs in a batch on the trunk of a tree, generally poplar. These eggs are covered in a white secretion which makes them into a

White Satin Moth

smooth white crust very like rice paper.

The young larvae hibernate and feed up in the spring. The larva is black and reddish brown and slightly hairy. On its back is a row of bright white patches. During the day-time the larva rests on the main trunk, and moves on to the leaves to feed at night.

The pupae are very hairy, and are formed in a very slight web, either among leaves or in a crevice in the bark.

The larvae will feed on poplar, willow, and sallow. In the country this species is hard to find, but it is common in some suburban districts and abundant in the Lea Valley and Lea Bridge Road, where it can be seen sitting on the trunks of poplars bordering the road. Young larvae are highly parasitized by a Braconid fly which makes a small yellow, egg-like cocoon.

If, however, the larger and more healthy larvae are collected when they are nearly fully grown, they should produce sound chrysalides which will ultimately hatch out.

BLACK ARCHES

Family LYMANTRIIDAE   *Lymantria monacha*

The female is illustrated; the male is similar
but smaller. Both sexes can vary a lot in colour,
and the most extreme forms are practically
black all over.

The moth emerges in late July and August, and
flies only at night. It is possible to find it by
searching tree trunks during the day.

The eggs are deposited in crevices in the bark
of trees and do not hatch until the following
spring.

The larvae are whitish or grey or sometimes a
curious green colour; they have black spots down
the sides and back with tufts of hair, and a dark
line running down their back. This line is not
continuous, however, and is broken by a patch of
the ground colour near the middle.

The larvae feed on oak, but will also feed on
elm, lime, birch, apple, aspen, and various
conifers.

The easiest way to obtain the larvae is to beat
the branches of oaks in June.

Black Arches

The pupa is shiny, metallic, and hairy; the ground colour is brown. It is enclosed in a slight web, generally in a crevice on bark.

The moth is fairly well distributed, but more common in the larger oak woods in the southern counties.

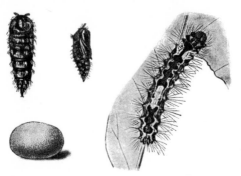

There are few species which make a hairy chrysalis, as shown above, but these are all very handsome to look at. Unfortunately their beautiful iridescence cannot be reproduced here.

There appears to be no satisfactory scientific explanation as to why these few species should be ornamented in this manner.

LACKEY MOTHS

Family LASIOCAMPIDAE

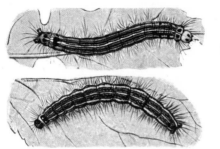

The species, which is illustrated by the left-hand figure overleaf, is common in many areas. It occurs amongst open common lands rather than in densely wooded areas.

The moth emerges in July and August, but is not a species you can easily find. The larvae are much more likely to attract attention.

The moth lays her eggs in a collar round a twig, and these remain through the winter and hatch at the end of April. The young larva makes a web tent and keeps moving to a fresh one after each skin change.

The fully grown larva is blue-grey, with narrow reddish stripes down its back and sides, and with a thin white line down the middle of its back. It is slightly hairy.

The pupa is formed inside a cocoon, and when the larva constructs this it spits a fluid on the silk inside, which dries to a yellow powder. The larva

Lackey Moths

Lackey
Malacosoma neustria

Ground Lackey
Malacosoma castrensis

feeds on a variety of trees and also rose, bramble, and several other plants.

The species illustrated by the right-hand figure above is very like the Common Lackey, but inhabits an entirely different type of country. It is found on salt marshes, mostly along the estuaries of rivers in the southern counties.

The times of appearance are the same as those just mentioned, and the larvae are very similar, but their web is flattish and practically on the ground. The larvae have no thin white line down their backs. (See lower figure on previous page.)

The larvae feed on any of the salt-marsh plants except grasses. Both the lackey moth larvae are very fast-walking when fully grown.

The eggs can survive immersion by salt water during the extreme tides in the spring.

Although found in such a distinctive habitat with its own specialized types of plants the larva can easily be reared in captivity if fed on apple or hawthorn.

PALE OAK EGGAR

Family LASIOCAMPIDAE   *Trichiura crataegi*

Male   Female

The Pale Oak Eggar is found in most well-wooded districts. The moth emerges in August and September and lays its eggs in a batch along a twig. These are protected by hairs from the body of the female, and they do not hatch until the following spring.

The young larvae hatch at irregular intervals, so that they can be found in varying stages of development. The larvae have several forms, some of which are very beautiful. The usual colour is black, with yellow collars between the segments and red spots in pairs down the back. Sometimes the yellow is replaced by white. The larvae are slightly hairy.

The larvae feed on hawthorn, blackthorn, oak, sallow, and several other trees. The pupa is inside a cocoon formed in a twig. These cocoons are rather like an acorn, rounded at each end and quite hard.

In the extreme northern counties and in Scotland this species will generally take two years

Pale Oak Eggar

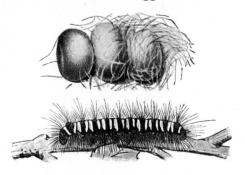

over its life-cycle, the first winter being passed as an egg and the second as a larva.

The specimens on page 119 are male and female. The male being slightly smaller.

After such fine and sometimes very colourful larvae which, when fully developed, are quite sizable caterpillars, the moth may seem a little disappointing. Fortunately this only happens with comparatively few species of moths.

Larvae can, however, be preserved in collections. Briefly, the method is to kill and squeeze out the contents and inflate them with a pointed glass tube. While inflated, dry them in a tin oven heated by a spirit lamp until they are rigid. They can then be mounted on a twig or wire.

DECEMBER MOTH

Family LASIOCAMPIDAE   *Poecilocampa populi*

The specimen figured has a worn appearance, but this is normal and due to the thinly scaled wings of this species.

The male and female are similar but the male is much smaller.

The moth is on the wing at the end of October, sometimes as late as December, and can be seen flying round street lamps at night. The species is fairly well distributed in England and Scotland.

The eggs, which are laid in the autumn, hatch in April, and the larvae feed on oak, hawthorn, elm, poplar, birch, and other trees.

The larvae are not easy to identify, as they have several forms. They can be black with red spots down their back and slightly hairy, or grey with a diamond pattern of dark brown running down the back. The ground colour is sometimes grey, with black and orange triangles down the back, or sometimes grey all over.

The pupa is a shiny red-brown, in a cocoon formed in a protected position under bark or amongst loose rubbish.

Although found mostly in actual woods or in well-wooded countryside, the moth can also be

December Moth

Male

Female

found in quite treeless districts. It is very
widely distributed, but never seems to occur in
any great numbers. From time to time numbers
appear together at light, especially round
mercury vapour lamps, but it is not easy to
choose a good night for collecting at the time of
year when this species is on the wing.

SMALL EGGAR

Family LASIOCAMPIDAE   *Eriogaster lanestris*

This moth, which is very like the one just described, cannot be confused with it, as it flies at quite a different time of year. The Small Eggar emerges early in the spring from cocoons which have overwintered, and lays its eggs in February and March.

The larvae are black, with rather square brown blotches down each side. These have a yellow margin to them. The larvae are slightly hairy. In the early stages they make a web tent in which they stay during wet weather or during a moult.

The larvae feed on blackthorn, hawthorn, plum and apple and cultivated varieties of these trees. The fully grown larvae leave the web and wander about to feed.

The pupa forms inside a typical eggar cocoon, like an acorn, rounded at each end and yellowish in colour. It will sometimes stay more than one winter within the cocoon. Although this occurs with many other species, this one does it more frequently and with a much higher proportion of the brood.

The Small Eggar is common in some areas, mostly in the southern and eastern counties.

The female, which is illustrated on the previous page, has a large tuft of hairs on the tip of its abdomen; these are shed during egg laying when they stick over the batch of eggs and help to camouflage them.

The Gipsy Moth and Gold-tail also use this method of concealing their eggs.

OAK EGGAR MOTH

Family LASIOCAMPIDAE   *Lasiocampa quercus*

A widely distributed species over most of the British Isles. In the south the species passes the winter as a hibernating larva, but in the north the first winter is spent as a larva and the second as a pupa which will emerge in the spring.

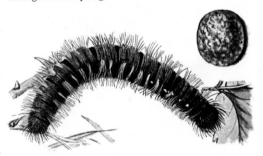

Largely on these grounds and because of the colour of the moths, which is much darker, these northern specimens are classified as a different species and referred to as the Northern Eggar with the Latin name of *Lasiocampa callunae*, although it can only be a different race and not a separate species.

The male and female are illustrated; the female is very much larger and pale buff in colour.

The larvae feed as soon as they wake from hibernation, and this is the easiest way to find them. Search a sunny bank in the spring, before there is too much herbage, and the larva will be found sunning themselves on twigs or bare patches of earth.

The larvae feed on a variety of trees and plants, but always low down. They will eat blackthorn, hawthorn, viburnum, dogwood, ivy, and ling.

Oak Eggar Moth

Male

Female

The moth is on the wing in late July and flies both in the afternoon and at night. This is one of the best species to watch, to see the females attracting the males by means of their scent glands.

The larvae grow to a fine size and are brown, furry, and with black bands separating the segments. They coil up when disturbed, and then these black rings are stretched and are more conspicuous.

The cocoon is made amongst leaves and is hard, yellowish, and rounded at each end.

GRASS EGGAR MOTH

Family LASIOCAMPIDAE   *Lasiocampa trifolii*

Male

Female

The Grass Eggar is much more restricted in its habitat than the Oak Eggar, and is found on coastal sand dunes or shingle wastes. Those found on the Kent coast are a pale yellow or buff and those found on the Lancashire coast and elsewhere are a dull, almost brick red in colour.

The moth is on the wing in August and lays its eggs in very small batches on leaves very near the ground. These hatch in the autumn and the young larvae hibernate while very small.

The larvae will feed on a variety of plants, chiefly grasses, kidney-vetch, and broom. They

feed almost on the ground and can be found
when fully grown sunning themselves on a warm
day.

The larvae are like those of the Oak Eggar, but
quite a different colour. They are a golden
brown, with black markings.

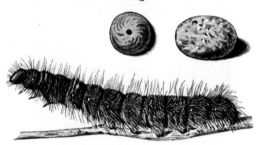

The cocoon is pale yellow, hard, and rounded
at either end, and formed amongst loose rubbish
on the ground.

The moth flies during the day but will also
fly at night; the male comes easily to a strong
light.

Like the Oak Eggar this species assembles
well. This is done by hanging a muslin bag
containing a freshly emerged female in the
afternoon and males will soon be attracted, sometimes in large numbers.

There is a variety which occurs in both sexes
in which the moth has the fore-wing bands
missing and is a uniform colour all over.

FOX MOTH

Family LASIOCAMPIDAE   *Macrothylacia rubi*

The Fox Moth is common on almost every wide stretch of heather on commons and moorland. It can be seen flying very erratically and at great speeds, low over the ground and gener-

ally in the early afternoon, during May and early June.

The female lays its eggs in a batch, on a twig or grass stalk, and these are very like the withered blooms of ling.

The male is illustrated on the next page; the female is similar, but larger and almost grey.

The larvae when small are dark brown, almost black, with bright golden bands round the body. When fully grown they are a chestnut brown with black markings.

The larvae are fully grown by the autumn and can be seen sunning themselves and walking about over short downland turf. They hibernate until the spring, wake up and sun themselves again, and move about before making their long, hairy cocoons.

Fox Moth

It is virtually impossible to collect fully grown larvae in the autumn and keep them yourself through the winter.

The larvae feed on heather, ling, bilberry, bramble and rose.

They pupate on the ground; often the cocoon will be under a flat stone or piece of tin lying on the ground. Larvae kept during the winter die, probably from a fungus disease, but now and then a collector succeeds in bringing a number through.

The safer method is to collect larvae during the first sunny days of spring when they will wake up and wander about before making their cocoons. They do not require food at this stage.

Messrs. H. F. and P. Robinson have succeeded in hatching the moth in the autumn by first treating the larvae in a refrigerator for a few weeks and then taking them out and slowly warming them up to room temperature.

DRINKER MOTH

Family LASIOCAMPIDAE   *Philudoria potatoria*

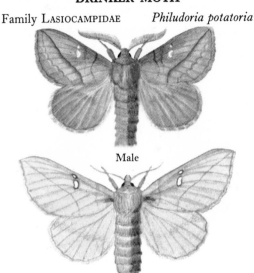

Male

Female

The Drinker derives its name from the fact
that the larvae, although feeding on grasses and
reeds, will drink great beads of dew or raindrops.

The male is smaller than the female and is
a light chestnut brown. There are varieties
however, and you can find yellow males and
dark brown females.

The moth is very widespread and abundant
in marshy areas in flat country where there are

Drinker Moth

dykes filled with reeds. The males come very readily to light, often in great numbers.

On a still night in the fens I have heard the larvae eating the crisp leaves of reeds.

The moth flies in July and lays its eggs on the food-plants. The young larvae hibernate while quite small and feed again in the spring. The fully grown larva looks very large for the moth it will ultimately produce.

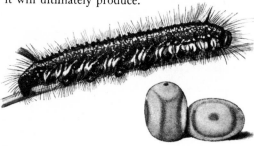

The fully grown larva is greyish black and covered with small yellow dots. It is hairy, and there is a small dense tuft of hairs at the head and tail.

The pupa is in a cocoon which is fastened to a reed or grass-stalk, and this is yellow and roughly pointed at both ends.

One of the easiest ways to obtain this species is to search a reed-filled ditch with a torch, during a June night, when the larvae will be large and well up on the stalks.

LAPPET MOTHS

Family LASIOCAMPIDAE

The Small Lappet was once fairly common over the stretches of bilberry-covered moorland at Cannock Chase and elsewhere, but is now regarded as virtually extinct. The species is found on the Continent, but not in great numbers.

The moth emerges in April, having spent the winter in the chrysalis state. The moth flies only at night,

and lays its eggs in small batches on the bilberry, on which the larva feeds.

The larva is not easy to describe. It is brown, sometimes grey or reddish brown, smooth along the back but hairy round the feet and along the lower parts of the sides.

The front or proper legs look fat and furry, and seen from above this is quite a good character for identification.

The pupa is black and formed inside a rather rough silk cocoon roughly pointed at both ends and pinkish grey in colour.

This species passes the winter as a pupa, but the Large Lappet hibernates as a larva.

The Lappet moth has the distinction of producing one of the largest larvae, next to the Death's Head Hawk, but the moth itself is also of great interest. When at rest the fore-wings are folded upwards over its back and the hind-wings then protrude and are only slightly drawn in. The effect, with its colouring and serrated outline, is exactly like a few dead beech leaves.

Lappet Moths

Small Lappet (male)
Epicnaptera ilicifolia

Lappet (female)
Gastropacha quercifolia

The moth emerges in July, flies at night, and lays its eggs in small, scattered batches. These eggs are beautifully ringed and are white and grey; there is no other egg like them.

The larvae when young are grey or brown or reddish brown, sometimes nearly black. They are hairy along the lower parts of their sides and round their feet. When on a twig they are almost impossible to see. When they extend their heads they reveal two bright orange bars close to the head.

In the later stages, after hibernation, these are replaced by two bluish-black bars. The larva may assume other colours, sometimes being marked with white as if flour had been dusted on the back.

EMPEROR MOTH

Family SATURNIIDAE　　　　*Saturnia pavonia*

Male

Female

The Emperor Moth appears to have two types of favourite haunt, one on open heath and moorland, and the other on waste ground along river estuaries, dyke banks, etc., where the larvae will be on low-growing blackthorn bushes.

The moth emerges during April and May, and can be seen flying on sunny afternoons.

The female lays her eggs in a batch on blackthorn or on heather; they look like the dead blooms of ling.

Emperor Moth

The young larva is blackish, but in the later stages is one of our more handsome insects. The fully grown larva is green, and round the stoutest part of each segment is a black band. Running round these bands is a row of small bulbs, sometimes yellow or alternatively pinkish mauve. From each of the bulbs there rises a tuft of black bristles.

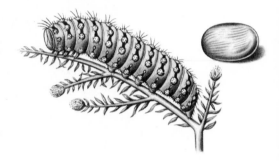

Besides heather and blackthorn the larvae will eat bramble, and in captivity will readily eat willow.

The cocoon is brown, hard, and made with rather coarse silk fibres and pointed at one end. This is the end from which the perfect insect will ultimately emerge, and while it can push out through this end, nothing can enter.

These cocoons can sometimes be seen lying on bare tracks through heather, where rooks have found them and split them open to get at the pupa during the winter months.

HOOK-TIP MOTHS

Family DREPANIDAE

OAK HOOK-TIP MOTH

A fairly common species in the southern counties, where it occurs in oak woods. The male is illustrated on the next page; the female is larger and paler, especially the hind wings.

The moth emerges during May and lays its eggs on the leaves of oaks. The larva feeds in

June and pupates, to emerge as a second brood in July and early August. The second-brood larvae feed in September, and the winter is passed in the pupal stage.

Hook-tip larvae hold their tails, which are pointed, cocked in the air, and are green with a saddle-mark on the back of yellowish colour.

The easiest way to collect this species is by beating the larvae from the oak branches.

Hook-Tip Moths

Scarce Hook-tip
Drepana harpagula

Oak Hook-tip
Drepana binaria

SCARCE HOOK-TIP

Since this species appears to live only on the one food-plant, the small-leaved lime, this may account for its extreme rarity and also for the very limited number of localities where it may be found.

The moth emerges in the spring and lays its eggs on the leaves of the lime. The larva takes some time to develop although it is so small.

The only way to obtain this rare moth with any degree of certainty is to attract males to lights placed under the trees.

Both male and female are the same size and very similar, but the female is a little darker in colour.

The male is shown above (left).

PEBBLE HOOK-TIP MOTH

Barred Hook-tip
Drepana cultraria

Pebble Hook-tip
Drepana falcataria

The Pebble Hook-tip is the largest of the small hook-tip family, and the example shown above (right) is a dark male, the normal male colouring being much more yellow. The female is larger and about the same colour as the male illustrated.

It is also the commonest of the family, and is widely distributed all over the British Isles.

The moth emerges in early May and again at the end of July. The larvae feed on birch during June and pupates, to emerge as a second brood is passed in the pupal stage. The small larvae feed in a pocket made by turning a leaf over along one edge and securing it with silk. When nearly fully grown they leave this shelter, and at that stage may be collected by beating the branches.

BARRED HOOK-TIP MOTH

The female of this species is shown on p. 139 (left); the male is similar, slightly smaller and with rather less pink colour on the bands.

The distribution of the species is governed by the chalk soil on which beeches—the food-plant —like to grow.

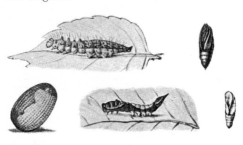

The moth emerges in May and again in August as a second brood. The winter is passed in the pupal stage.

The larvae feed on the leaves of beech during June and again in August, and they can be obtained by beating the branches of this tree.

SCALLOPED HOOK-TIP MOTH

Male   Female

Scalloped Hook-tip
Drepana lacertinaria

The moth of this species is easily distinguished from all the rest of this family by the scallops along the edges of the fore-wings.

The female is slightly larger than the male and lighter in colour.

The moth emerges in early May and again late in July, and is widely distributed, but scarcer in parts of the north.

The larvae feed on birch during June and September, and the winter is passed in the pupal stage.

The larvae feed in the manner just described for the previous species, but during the day rest exposed on top of the leaves; they can thus be collected by beating the branches.

CHINESE CHARACTER MOTH

Male   Female
Chinese Character (*Cilix glaucata*)

The Chinese Character when at rest folds
its wings over its back, and the black and white
markings then closely resemble a bird-dropping
on a leaf. The moth is widespread in its distribution, but gets scarcer towards the north.

The moth is on the wing in early May and
again in August, and the easiest way to see this
species is to catch it while it flies along hedge-
rows at dusk.

The larvae feed on blackthorn and hawthorn,
and also on apple and pear.

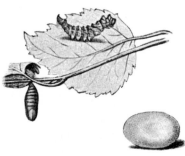

GREEN SILVER LINES

Family HYLOPHILIDAE   *Bena fagana*

Male   Female

CREAM-BORDERED GREEN PEA

Family HYLOPHILIDAE   *Earias clorana*

Green Silver Lines is a pretty species and is fairly common in oak woods and widely distributed.

The moth is on the wing in June and July, and lays its eggs on the leaves of oak, birch, nut, and beech, on which the larva will feed.

The larvae feed during August and September, and are not easy to find. The species is most easily obtained by disturbing the branches of oaks at the right time, when the moth will fly out.

The cocoons are also boat-shaped and a pinkish brown, generally fastened under a leaf, but sometimes on bark or elsewhere.

Green Silver Lines

Both the male and female are shown on p. 143; the female is the same size as the male, but not quite such a bright green, the colour being yellowish green.

Cream-bordered Green Pea

This is the smallest of this little family, but it is a most attractive moth and quite common in suitable localities. The larva feeds on willows, especially osier. It is common in the fens and on the Norfolk Broads, and is also found commonly on Romney Marsh.

The moth flies in June and early July, and the larvae feed during August and September. Sometimes there is a partial second brood.

The larva feeds in the shoot at the end of a branch, and spins a few leaves together. The cocoon is a curious boat-shaped structure fastened to a twig or on the trunk of the tree, and the winter is passed in this stage.

SCARCE SILVER LINES

Family HYLOPHILIDAE   *Pseudoips bicolorana*

This is the largest of this family, and when freshly emerged is a beautiful insect.

It is widely distributed and possibly rather more common in the large oak woods in the southern counties.

Although it is well distributed it does not appear to be common, and it is a difficult species to come across. It can sometimes be found at rest on the trunks of oaks, and sometimes a specimen will come to a light.

The moth flies in July and lays its eggs on the leaves of oaks. The larvae, unlike those of the others in this family, spend the winter in the larval stage and do not pupate until the following June.

The cocoon is boat-shaped with a small keel along the top. At the head end this keel is raised and is really in two halves. When the moth pushes its way out, this opens like a slit and closes again, and no join can be seen.

The chrysalis inside the cocoon is pale green, with a thin black line down the back.

The male and female are about the same size and colour.

The cocoon, illustrated on p. 145, shows the keel like the underside of a boat with the bow pointing downwards. The colour is pinky brown.

This species does not vary, but there have been a few remarkable varieties recorded in which the fore-wings have red or reddish markings added.

In 1951 a specimen was captured in a light trap in the London Zoo.

You should be careful when killing moths which are green in colour. This group just described are fairly easy, but the "emerald" family are more difficult, as the green colour is easily changed to brown by a cyanide bottle or ammonia.

The safest way is to use a small hypodermic syringe with ethyl acetate. Earlier collectors used a mapping-pen dipped in oxalic acid and inserted this below the thorax on the underside, but this method of killing is not recommended.

WHITE ERMINE MOTH

Family ARCTIIDAE   *Spilosoma lubricipeda*

Scottish form

This is a widely distributed and very common moth, found in most types of country, including gardens. The moth can be seen in June sitting about during the day, on fences and posts.

The female is shown above; the male is similar, but usually with more and larger black dots. Those found in Scotland have the fore-wings brownish. The extent of variation of the spots is considerable in this species. They can be almost absent or much larger and joined in lines.

The moth lays its eggs in a batch on leaves of low-growing plants. The larvae will feed on practically any low-growing plant, and are brown with long hairs and a reddish-orange stripe down the middle of their backs. They can often be seen early in September crawling rapidly across country roads.

The pupa is formed inside a strong silk cocoon into which the hairs from the larva are spun, and this is generally fastened in a secure corner to spend the winter.

This moth will come readily to a light and flies into houses and round lamp-posts. Fences under lamp-posts are the best places to search for specimens, as they will be attracted there at night and remain at rest by day.

The Water Ermine, *Spilosoma urticae*, now virtually extinct in Britain, has fewer spots on the fore-wings and none on the hind-wings.

BUFF ERMINE MOTH

Family ARCTIIDAE   *Spilosoma lutea*

This species is very like the White Ermine, but the fore-wings and hind-wings are buff-coloured and the spots larger. There are also black spots on the hind-wings.

The male and female are very similar, but the female has bolder black spots down the body.

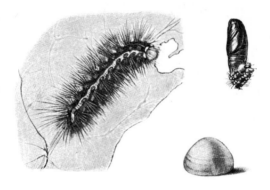

This species has many varieties, usually with the spots elongated to form thin black lines, but there are extreme forms where the whole ground-colour is black and the veins are left buff. In these specimens the head and body remain unchanged.

The moths emerge in June and lay their eggs on the leaves of low-growing plants, on which the larvae feed.

Buff Ermine Moth

The larva is very like that of the White Ermine, the line down the back being present but not so pronounced, and there is also a yellowish or greyish-white line down each side of the body.

The pupa, which is formed inside a cocoon amongst rubbish on the ground, is not as dark as that of the White Ermine and is a glossy reddish brown.

The moth is very common over most of the British Isles.

Normally this species has only one brood during the year, but if kept in captivity you can generally manage to obtain two broods in one year. No doubt by using a refrigerator to produce an artificial winter and keeping larvae warm in cold weather you could increase this to three or even four broods. This is invaluable if you are experimenting with varieties.

MUSLIN MOTH

Family ARCTIIDAE   *Cycnia mendica*

Male   Female

The Muslin Moth is a very common species and found all over the British Isles. The sexual dimorphism is so great that both sexes have been illustrated above.

In Ireland there is found a form in which the male is buff all over. There are also varieties of the female which can occur anywhere, having the spots elongated into lines or short thick bars.

The moth flies in May and June, and will lay its eggs anywhere, for instance upon wire-netting which it has flown into at night. For some reason or other you can be certain of finding lines of eggs laid on the old type of string netting surrounding tennis courts.

The larvae will eat practically any low-growing plant, and also shoots of elder.

The larvae are not quite so well covered with hairs as the previous few species, and are brownish grey in colour with pale-brown hairs. The hairs grow from greyish-ringed pale-brown warts.

Muslin Moth

The pupa is dark brown, nearly black, and is shiny. It is formed in a silk cocoon incorporating the hairs from the larva.

During the end of July and the early weeks of August you can be certain of seeing larvae of the Muslin Moth, fully grown, running about on

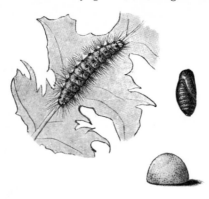

footpaths and roads, even in built-up areas, but generally one at a time. They can move extraordinarily fast if the day is warm. The larvae running about in this manner are not worth collecting as they frequently prove to be parasitized. It is better to collect a number from one plant or small area.

CLOUDED BUFF MOTH

Family ARCTIIDAE   *Diacrisia sannio*

The Clouded Buff is well distributed over the British Isles, but nowhere is it found in great numbers. There are small areas where it is fairly common, but it is a difficult species to obtain.

Both sexes are illustrated on the following page, and the species is not given to extreme variation.

The moth flies in June, and there is only one brood in a year. In captivity, this species will have up to five or six broods in a year, if kept warm and fed on dandelion leaves.

The larvae feed on plantains, dandelion, and dock, and hibernate while quite small; in the spring they feed again.

The larva is reddish brown and covered with brown hairs. There is a yellow-and-white stripe

Clouded Buff Moth

Male

Female

along the back and two fairly dark stripes along the sides.

The pupa, which is formed in May, is inside a rather thinly constructed cocoon on the ground.

This species is not given to extreme variation but would be worth breeding experimentally, owing to the number of broods obtainable by controlled temperatures. The male sometimes occurs with the hind-wing bands absent.

The male can sometimes be found flying on sunny days, but otherwise this species flies only at night.

RUBY TIGER MOTH

Family ARCTIIDAE   *Phragmatobia fuliginosa*

This species occurs all over the British Isles, but specimens from the north are very much darker. Those found further south are a brighter red, especially on the hind-wings. Those found in Scotland have the hind-wings practically black all over; one of these is shown above (right).

There is a very rare form in which the red colouring is replaced by yellow.

This has been bred once only in this country to my knowledge, but unfortunately the collector was called away by a sudden emergency and his stock perished. Most of the series he bred are now in the national collection.

The moth emerges in May and June, and lays its eggs in batches on dock, plantains and other low-growing plants. The young larvae hibernate and feed up in the following spring.

In some years there is a partial second brood, and up to three broods can be produced in captivity.

One of the best ways to secure this species is

to find the larvae in the spring, when they will sit about on banks on warm sunny days.

The larvae are black when fully grown and covered with fairly dense hairs. These almost obscure a reddish line which runs along the back.

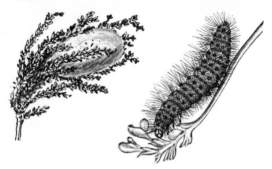

The pupa is made inside a silk cocoon amongst dead stalks or leaves, generally off the ground.

Richard South records the caterpillar of this species as possessing a remarkable vitality and states that one was embedded in ice for fourteen days at least, becoming active in less than half an hour after the ice around it melted, and the same larva pupated not long afterwards. Most lepidopterous larvae stand cold fairly well during the winter but long periods of wet during this time of the year are very harmful to hibernating larvae.

WOOD TIGER MOTH

Family ARCTIIDAE   *Parasemia plantaginis*

The wood Tiger is well distributed, but is often confined to fairly well-defined colonies, generally on the chalk downs in the south and on moors and hills further north. It is fairly common in some years and scarce in others.

On most specimens there is a well-formed swastika on each fore-wing. The female is

darker than the male, and the body is red, but I have seen a few examples where the body is yellow, and they appear to be uncommon and worth watching for. The moths fly during the day.

The eggs are laid on the leaves of very low-growing plants. The larvae feed on plantains, common rock-rose and salad burnet, and can be seen basking on sunny days, often on bare earth, mole-hills, ant-hills, and even waste paper. Although called the Wood Tiger, the larvae are found right out on open ground, often in bleak situations.

The moth is on the wing in May and June, and

Wood Tiger Moth

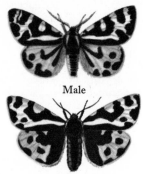

Male

Female

the young larvae hibernate and feed up in the spring. They are greyish, with fairly dense black hairs.

An interesting variety of this moth has the ground colour of all wings white and is called var. *hospita*, Schiff. This is found in the Lake District on the Langdale Pikes, but it is more easily obtained in Scotland.

A much rarer form has the fore-wings nearly all black, and other forms have the black bars and spots joined on the hind-wings in the male, while the female has the hind-wings practically all black.

GARDEN TIGER MOTH

Family ARCTIIDAE   *Arctia caja*

The Garden Tiger is probably one of our better-known moths, since it can be seen sitting about in the day and flying round lamps at night, and its larvae, which can sometimes be seen crawling rapidly across roads and open ground on hot days, are the well-known "woolly bears".

The species is well distributed and can be collected as larvae in the spring, when, after hibernation, the young larvae sit about and sun themselves on the ground or on low herbage.

The larvae will sometimes appear in large numbers, and this occurred in recent years on many bomb-sites.

The larvae will eat practically anything. They are extremely furry, the hairs being long. They are mostly black, with reddish or ginger hairs at the sides. The tips of the long black hairs are white. These larvae are quite unmistakable, and no others have such fine coats. They are able to move quite fast across open ground.

Garden Tiger Moth

The larva pupates in a rather flimsy silk cocoon, and the dried skin of the larva can be seen on the tip of the pupa.

The moth emerges in early July, but in captivity, if fed on cabbage in a dark cupboard, the species will be continuously brooded and several

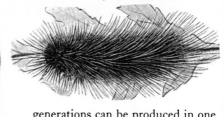

generations can be produced in one year.

Many extraordinary varieties of this species have been produced, ranging from all black to all cream, and more commonly, with all-chocolate forewings and with huge black spots, joined together, on the hind-wings. The colouring of male and female is identical, but the latter is much larger.

CREAM-SPOT TIGER MOTH

Family ARCTIIDAE   *Arctia villica*

This is also a common species, but is not found quite so often in gardens and built-up districts. It is more often seen in the perfect or adult state sitting on leaves on the edge of a wood or on a bank. The moth emerges in June, and can be seen flying on sunny afternoons

and also round lamps at night. It can often be found during the day-time sitting on fences close to street or other lamps.

The moth lays beautiful pearly batches of eggs on the leaves of low-growing plants.

The young larvae are very furry and are black in the early stages. They hibernate and can be seen in the spring sunning themselves on bare patches of earth on banks. Roadside banks are not very good hunting-grounds unless the road is of flint or otherwise untarred. The black larvae make one final moult in the spring, when

Cream-Spot Tiger Moth

the last stage will be a dark-brown larva with the head, feet and claspers reddish.

The larvae will eat dandelion, nettle, dock, plantain and many other wild and garden plants.

The pupa is formed inside a rather flimsy silk cocoon amongst leaves or rubbish. Both the pupae of the Cream-spot and Garden Tiger moths are rather delicate to handle.

The female is much the same as the male. The amount of black on the hind-wings varies in some examples, and there is a form, which is found wild from time to time, in which the forewings have a large cream patch near and extending to the edge of the fore-wings.

The species is widely distributed, but more common in the southern counties. The adults come well to light traps, especially mercury vapour, when they can be taken in numbers during late June and early July.

JERSEY TIGER MOTH

Family ARCTIIDAE   *Euplagia quadripunctaria*

This handsome species is more or less confined to the county of Devonshire, where it occurs
in colonies in several places.

The moth emerges during August, and can be
seen flying both by day and night. The eggs
are laid on low-growing plants.

The larvae hibernate while they are still
extremely small, and continue feeding in the
spring. They are hairy and black, with an
orange stripe down the back and with creamy-

white spots on the sides. Like others of this family, they can most easily be found whilst basking in the sunshine.

The larvae will feed on honeysuckle, bramble, groundsel, dandelion, white dead-nettle and several other plants. They make a flimsy silken cocoon down amongst dead leaves and rubbish on the ground.

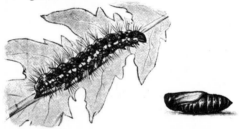

The adult moth, which comes fairly easily to a lamp at night, has an alternative form, the lower illustration on page 163, in which the red colouring on the wings is replaced by yellow; there are also intermediate pinkish-orange forms.

Unlike other tiger moths this species has not yet produced a wide range of varieties, possibly because it is not quite so easy to find or breed. The small isolated cream spot of the costal edge of the fore-wing is sometimes absent.

SCARLET TIGER MOTH

Family ARCTIIDAE   *Panaxia dominula*

Although fairly common and fairly widely
distributed over England and Scotland, this is not
a species you would easily find unless you happened
to chance on a colony or deliberately searched in
one of its known haunts.

The species occurs in colonies, often along
river-banks and in other marshy places.

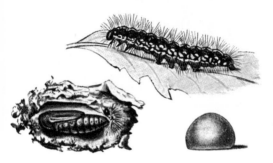

The moth emerges in July and lays its eggs
loose or scattered about in very small batches.
The young larvae hibernate and feed up in the
spring. The larvae feed on stinging-nettle,
comfrey, bramble and blackthorn, as well as
several other low-growing plants.

The larvae are quite distinctive, being black,
slightly hairy, and with yellow patches down the
back and sides. There are also small blue or
white dots on the black portions of the body.
There is only the one brood in a year. The moth
flies at night.

Scarlet Tiger Moth

There used to be a well-known form of this moth in which the red colouring was replaced by yellow, but this has not been found in recent years and it will be interesting to see if it reappears. Several variations do occur, mostly having the fore-wings nearly black all over. Careful breeding in captivity has produced entirely black specimens. One of the rare forms worth watching for is ab. *juncta*, in which the two orange spots on the fore-wing become joined to form one long one.

By selection you can get the centre spots to go, leaving the small outer marginal spots and the two large spots nearest the thorax.

A further stage leaves you with only the two large basal spots, and this is called *bimacula;* but it is very hard to go a stage further and get these to go. For those who are interested some very fine coloured plates of the varieties of this species may be found in the proceedings of The British Entomological and Natural History Society.

CINNABAR MOTH

Family ARCTIIDAE *Callimorpha jacobaeae*

This is probably the most common of our day-flying moths and well known to many who walk through rough grassy ground during June.

Most people no doubt know the larvae, but probably without knowing what these larvae will produce.

The larvae are the black- and orange-banded caterpillars found feeding on the flowers of ragwort during July, August and sometimes September. Country folk call them "wort maggots with football jerseys on."

Their bright orange bands serve as a warning to birds that they are extremely distasteful. If you throw a few to a tame robin he will disregard them, but stain some green and he will attack them at once, only to leave them and wipe his beak on discovering their flavour.

In some localities these larvae are often very abundant and devour the whole flowerhead of every ragwort plant in a field.

In gardens they will feed on groundsel, and the fully grown larvae turn into small reddish

Cinnabar Moth

pupae in the ground, sometimes a few centimetres down. Although the moth flies freely in sunshine it is also on the wing at night, and sometimes huge numbers will fly to a strong light.

From time to time a form occurs with the red colouring replaced by orange, but these are extremely rare. Another variety rather more

common than the orange form is a banded or confluent form where the red costal bar is continued round the wing-tip and joins up the two spots to form one continuous line.

The larvae have also been found with creamy white bands instead of orange, but only once so far. If you are fortunate enough to find more they should be handed to an expert so that their genetics can be studied.

COMMON FOOTMAN

Family ARCTIIDAE   *Eilema lurideola*

This species is very similar to several others in this small family, and has been selected because it is the one most frequently met with. The two other species which most closely resemble it are the Scarce and Northern Footman.

The Common Footman is well distributed all over the British Isles. It is on the wing in July, and can be seen sitting about on foliage or on fences, and will also fly to windows at night.

The other two species mentioned above are also about at the same time. In the Common Footman the yellow line along the top edge of the wing terminates with a point. In the Scarce Footman this line is continued to the fringe along the edge of the wing.

In the Northern Footman the line also continues to join the fringe, but the hind-wings are suffused with blackish markings as well.

The larva is greyish, covered with blackish hairs along the back and with yellowish hairs along the sides. There are three dark lines along the back and an orange stripe along part of the side.

Common Footman

Like others of this family, the larvae usually feed on lichen growing on the trunks and branches of trees, but they have also been found on sallows and other bushes on which there was no lichen growing, and in captivity they will eat sallow and apple.

The pupa forms in a cocoon amongst lichen, but remains like this for only a short time. The greater part of the year, including the winter months, is spent in the larval stage.

Some kinds of corrugated asbestos roofs, once they have become well weathered, grow a fine crop of small lichens and the Common Footman as well as larvae of the Marbled Beauty can be found in this situation. Specimens of the Common Footman have been captured in a light trap in the Zoological Gardens, Regents Park, and these have probably fed on lichen on buildings.

FOUR-SPOTTED FOOTMAN

Family ARCTIIDAE   *Lithosia quadra*

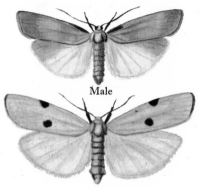

Male

Female

In spite of the name, the spots are carried only by the female, the fore-wings of the male being dark grey and having no spots.

There is also a Four-dotted Footman, but this is very much smaller and has small dots on the wings of both sexes.

The moth is the largest of this family and is generally found along the south coast. Its old haunt was the New Forest, where it used to be seen in great numbers, but there are not many to be found there at the present time.

As the illustrations show, the moth itself is quite distinctive. It is on the wing during July.

The larva is more easily separated from those

of other footmen by the four wavy yellow lines
along the back. It has a black shiny head and
grey and black hairs. The raised spots along
the back are red. The larvae feed on lichens,

mostly those on oak-trees, and they can be
obtained by jarring the lichen-covered branches
when the larvae are nearly fully grown in early
June. The larvae, which hatch from the egg in
August, hibernate through the winter and feed
again in the spring.

The moths do not come readily to ordinary
lights, but may sometimes be attracted to a sugar
patch. For those collectors who are fortunate
enough to possess a mercury vapour light this
species will be found to come in some numbers
during late July and early August. About three
weeks earlier the pretty Rosy Footman will, in
many districts, come in large numbers to this
type of light.

OLD LADY MOTH

Super-family AGROTIDES

Family CARADRINIDAE   *Mormo maura*

During the day you can often disturb this moth, which will rest behind curtains or in an outhouse or coal-shed. It comes out at dusk and flies up and down, not unlike a small bat.

The moth is on the wing during July and August, and lays her eggs in a batch on low-growing plants. The larvae, which grow to quite a good size, are brown with a darker diamond pattern down their backs. There are also some pale streaks placed obliquely along the sides.

The young larvae feed on low-growing plants and then hibernate for the winter. The following spring they will feed very much higher up, on the shoots of bushes of sallow, hawthorn, birch and hazel.

The fully grown larva pupates in the leaves on the ground, or sometimes a little way into loose soil.

The species is well distributed over the greater part of the British Isles, and is common in many places, often in suburban gardens. It has even been seen in the London area, flying along roads as well as in gardens.

This species forms one of the favourite foods of bats and you can find their wings in your porch in the morning, if you have a light showing through a window over the door.

The easiest way to obtain one is to sugar tree-trunks bordering country lanes or even trees in your garden. It can also be found at night feeding from the sweet-scented tresses of the buddleia bush.

Old Lady Moth

A rare variety of this species has a fine white border round each wing where the outer band is normally found.

During the last war I disturbed one of these fine varieties from under some tiles I was replacing after bombing. Unfortunately, as I was astride the coal-shed roof at the time I could not give chase. I tried sugaring in the garden around, but the moth did not return. Most moths have a favourite type of roosting place, and many will return to the same spot night after night.

I recently discovered a new place to examine, and that was the underside of a small concrete bridge which carried a road over a small stream. One morning there were eleven Old Ladies at roost, and I marked some of these with a small spot of bright quick-drying fluid, such as is used for correcting stencils. Nine of these were present the next day along with one new arrival.

RED UNDERWING

Family PLUSIIDAE   *Catocala nupta*

Although this is a beautiful moth you may
not see its colour until it flies away, since the
fore-wings hide the hind-wings completely when
at rest.

You can find this species at rest on old fences,
walls and on the trunks of poplar and willow
trees during the day-time in August and September, but their colouring makes them very hard to
spot.

The female lays her eggs on the trunks of
poplar and willow trees, and they do not hatch
until the following spring.

During the day the baby larvae rest on the
leaves, lying along the mid-rib. You can spot
these by standing under a pollard willow and
looking upwards. If you see a black line about
2 cm long in the middle of a leaf, during early
June, it will almost certainly be this larva.

Red Underwing

When the larvae are bigger they feed at night and rest on the trunk during the day, often wedged in a very small crevice. The larvae look very like stick caterpillars, but can easily be distinguished as their underneath has bold black spots down its whole length.

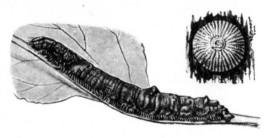

The pupa forms in the ground, inside a slight cocoon, often just at the foot of the tree, and has a greyish bloom over it which can be rubbed off with the fingers.

This species is common where there are poplars and willows, but it is quite nocturnal and can easily escape notice. You can obtain it by cycling slowly past old oak palings, if there are willows in the district, early in the morning before the sun shines on them.

They come very easily, sometimes in numbers, to treacle mixture placed on the trunks of willows.

LARGE YELLOW UNDERWING

Family CARADRINIDAE   *Triphaena pronuba*

This is one of our commonest moths, found almost everywhere. The moth can be disturbed from all kinds of roosting-places during the day, especially ivy growing on a wall, and it will also

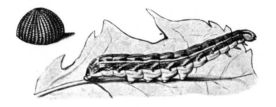

fly into the house at night and circle round the lights.

The moth is on the wing during June, July, and August, and is nocturnal. The female lays her eggs on almost any low-growing plant. The larva, which is difficult to distinguish from the many kinds in this group, feeds at night and during the day remains at the roots of plants. It will also feed at ground-level, especially in the spring after hibernation. It can be found in every garden and even on lawns round the crowns of dandelions.

The pupa, which is a bright reddish brown, is formed in the earth.

There are several other underwings in this family, all smaller except the Broad Bordered, which has a bold black border on the hind-wings much darker and wider than the one illustrated

Large Yellow Underwing

here. The species is not likely to be met with in gardens.

This species has been chosen to represent one of our largest families of moths, the Noctuids or night-flying species, or more recently referred to as the Agrotids. There are about three hundred and seventy species in this country and many of them have a wide range of variation so that correct identification for beginners is not easy, but many of the interesting life cycles make this a fascinating group for study.

You will find there is quite a considerable variation in the forms of the Large Yellow Underwing. Some of these are quite a fine red colour, and others will be almost yellow or light grey. You will also notice that some have a more or less uniform colour, while others have a more mottled pattern. This difference distinguishes the sexes. The figure above illustrates the male, and the pattern is clearly shown.

So far I have only seen one example which had the hind-wings a light cream colour. It was a bred specimen, so it could not have faded, and this form must be very rare.

GHOST SWIFT

Super-family MICROPTERYGES
Family HEPIALIDAE   *Hepialus humuli*

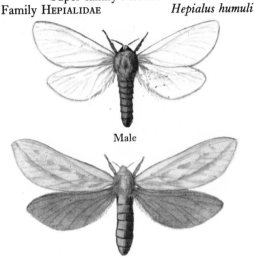

Male

Female

There are several swifts in this small family, but the
Ghost Swift is the largest, although not as common as
some of the smaller species.

The Ghost Swift gets its name from the white wings
of the male. The female is also shown above, and
both may be seen flying at dusk over rough grasslands.

The female lays her small dark eggs loose, as she
flies about, and the young larvae on hatching bore into
the ground and feed on the roots of grass and various
plants.

The larvae are long and thin and white, with a
slightly waxy appearance, and with brown heads.

Ghost Swift

They can be dug up with those of the Common Swift in gardens as well as uncultivated ground.

The pupa is formed in the earth, and is long for its size and roughened, with very short spikes which help it to wriggle to the surface before the moth emerges. The hatched cocoons may be seen stuck half in and half out of the soil during June.

The moth flies in July, and can be found all over the British Isles. The males of those found in the extreme north have dark markings on their wings. The larvae pass the winter feeding underground.

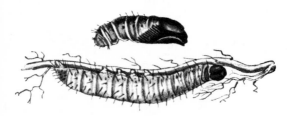

The easiest way to obtain one of this species is to catch it hovering over a plant on rough ground at dusk. You can try digging for larvae but it is exhausting work. The best places are clumps of grass, ragwort or artemesia growing on ground which has been cultivated and then allowed to go wild again.

The moths turn greasy extremely easily in the cabinet, so as soon as you set them remove the bodies while still on the drying-boards, and soak them in a suitable solvent such as toluene, giving at least two baths in clean tubes. They can then easily be glued in place as the setting-board will keep them in position.

LARGE EMERALD

Super-family GEOMETRIDES
Family GEOMETRIDAE   *Hipparchus papilionaria*

This is the largest of the emeralds and is quite common, especially where there is plenty of young birch and hazel, on which the larvae feed. It is found all over the British Isles except in the extreme north.

The moth itself is nocturnal, so may escape attention. The wings of specimens eaten by bats may often be seen alongside paths through wooded country during June and July.

The moth lays her eggs on the leaves or twigs of birch and hazel, and sometimes on alder, and the young larvae then hibernate and feed up in the spring. During the winter they get in a small piece of curled leaf, sometimes spun to a twig. Often the larvae will spend the winter attached to a silk pad spun on a shoot. The fully grown larva is green, with a tinge of red in some parts, and is stick-like but very fat for its size, which distinguishes it from other species.

The pupa is formed amongst dead leaves on the ground in a slight, silken cocoon.

Large Emerald

This and the next species are two representatives of a very large family, all of which have stick-like larvae with only two pairs of claspers at the tail. They can grip with these and stand with their front legs off the ground.

Unfortunately, like other members in this family, this Emerald loses its colour very easily and turns to the colour of the Swallow-tail moth. This can generally be avoided if the specimen is killed by injecting oxalic acid with a fine hypodermic needle. It should also be kept in the dark as soon as set. Even after being green for years a specimen will sometimes turn brown suddenly after exposure to light.

SWALLOW-TAILED MOTH

Family GEOMETRIDAE   *Ourapteryx sambucaria*

This is a very common moth which can be seen flying round lamp-posts at night; sometimes it comes into houses. It is nocturnal, and during the day can often be disturbed from ivy growing on walls, in which it roosts.

The moth is on the wing in July, and is common in most parts of England and Wales. It is widespread though uncommon in Scotland. The female lays her eggs, which turn scarlet, on the leaves of ivy and privet, and the larvae hibernate through the winter about half-grown.

The larva is brown, very long and thin, and one of the better examples of a stick-larva. They may be obtained by holding a sheet or beating tray under overhanging ivy and beating it, when the larvae are nearly fully grown in May or early June.

The pupa is suspended underneath a leaf by silken threads so that it hangs lengthwise and not from one end.

Swallow-Tailed Moth

There is little variation to be found in this species but there is a rare form in which the

bands are a little closer together and broadened so that they nearly join.   In this form the colour of the bands is darker and rather brown.

The species is one of our larger and more conspicuous geometrids and when the moth is at rest the wings are held flat to the resting surface and spread out.

GOAT MOTH

Super-family PSYCHES

Family COSSIDAE   *Cossus cossus*

The Goat Moth obtains its name from the
smell of both the larva and the moth and anything with which they come in contact. The
moth is common and widely distributed, but at
the same time localized by its feeding habits.

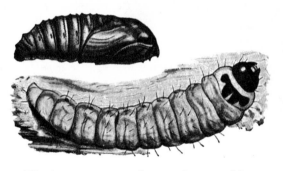

The larvae are more frequently met with, as
they will sometimes wander long distances from
their feeding-places before they make their cocoon
and pupate.

The moth flies at night during July, and lays
its eggs on a dead or dying willow or poplar tree,
though sometimes ash or oaks are selected. The
larva feeds on the decaying wood, boring
long tunnels and producing a quantity of sawdust
in the process. The larva makes a cocoon in
the autumn and hibernates. The following

Goat Moth

spring it will continue feeding. It may pass three winters in this manner. After its last hibernation the larva leaves its cocoon in the spring and shortly afterwards makes a fresh cocoon and pupates.

The larva when fully grown is one of our largest, and is bright pink along the back, yellow along the sides, and has a black head. It is also shiny and smooth. If you find one you should keep it in a metal container, since it can bore its way through thick wood. There are often many larvae together in one tree if conditions for them are suitable.

WOOD LEOPARD MOTH

Family COSSIDAE   *Zeuzera pyrina*

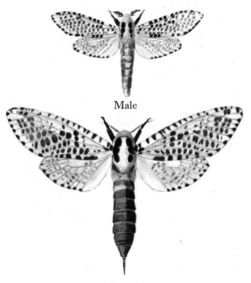

Male

Female

The Wood Leopard Moth is a near relation of
the last species, and is common in many districts
all over the British Isles.   It may possibly escape
attention since it is nocturnal and the larvae are
well concealed.

The moth is on the wing in July, and lays its
eggs in a crevice or under bark with a specially
long ovipositor in its tail.

Wood Leopard Moth

The larvae will feed by boring into the centre of branches, and will take two years to reach maturity if in an apple-tree or a hawthorn. In small sycamore trees about 2·5 cm in diameter, and also in lilac, they can grow to full size in one year.

They can be found in gardens and are common in some parts of central London, where they bore into plane trees. Sometimes their pellets of sawdust, bright red in colour, can be seen on the pavement at the foot of a tree.

One of the best ways to secure the moth is to search tree trunks during the month of emergence, when freshly emerged specimens will be drying their wings or sitting on the bark.

The larva is white, with black dots and with a black head.

Formerly this species was a pest in orchards, boring in fruit-trees and causing decay which caused branches laden with the weight of fruit to break off. The modern insecticides appear to have overcome this.

INDEX

INDEX